Real Learning

A Bridge to Cognitive Neuroscience

Harry Morgan

ScarecrowEducation
Lanham, Maryland • Toronto • Oxford
2003

Published in the United States of America
by ScarecrowEducation
An imprint of The Rowman & Littlefield Publishing Group, Inc.
4501 Forbes Boulevard, Suite 200, Lanham, Maryland 20706
www.scarecroweducation.com

PO Box 317
Oxford
OX2 9RU, UK

British Library Cataloguing in Publication Information Available

Library of Congress Cataloging-in-Publication Data

Morgan, Harry, 1926–
   Real learning : a bridge to cognitive neuroscience / Harry Morgan.–
1st ed.
     p. cm.
   Includes bibliographical references and index.
   ISBN 1-57886-063-6 (pbk. : alk. paper)
   1. Educational psychology. 2. Learning–Physiological aspects.
3. Cognitive neuroscience. I. Title.
LB1057 .M67 2003
370.15′2–dc21   2003011175

*Dedicated to
Stephen Jay Gould,
Citizen Scientist
1942–2002*

CONTENTS

ACKNOWLEDGMENTS

The model displayed in figure 5.1 is based in part on ideas originating from the work of R. C. Atkinson and R. M. Shiffrin, *Human Memory: A Proposed System and Its Control Processes*, in *The Psychology of Learning and Motivation: Advances in Research and Theory*, edited by K. W. Spence and J. T. Spence, 90–191 (New York: Academic Press, 1968). The figure displayed in Figure 4.1 is reproduced from Michael Shafto, *How We Know* (New York: HarperCollins Publishers, 1985).

INTRODUCTION

As the utopian tradition recognizes, we can often devise lovely and optimal systems in abstract principle, but then be utterly unable to apply them in practice because an imperfect world precludes their operation. The central logic of Darwinism faces an issue of this kind. The two essential biological postulates of natural selection—its operation at the organismal level and its creativity in crafting adaptations—build a sufficient theoretical apparatus to fuel the system. The play of evolution can run with such a minimal cast, but we do not know whether the drama can actually unfold on our planet until we also examine and specify the character of the theater—the geological and environmental stage for the play of natural selection.

—Stephen Jay Gould

This book is organized to focus on education theory and practice in six chapters—experience, attention, perception, acquiring knowledge, memory, and retrieval—and is designed to inform students and scholars about how learners acquire, organize, and use knowledge.

Education as an area of study is not considered a discipline, as are biology, chemistry, history, or mathematics, for example. This predicament in which education finds itself need not be viewed negatively, however. Some aspects of an unaligned status can even be viewed positively because certain freedoms can accompany open choices.

Scholars who implement education theory and practice are free to adopt what they consider most suitable, under self-determining conditions, without a binding commitment to a preselected dogma. For some time now, the field of education has expanded its theory and practice by modeling theories, principles, and practices from other disciplines.

When educators recognized the need to better understand the complex nature of learning, for example, they investigated theories emerging from psychological studies. In the early 1900s, this meant that educators modeled behaviorism because that approach was embraced by psychologists of that time. When educators attempted to translate behavioristic theory into educational practice, the results were not always desirable. This brought an avalanche of criticism over the next two decades, and behaviorism was modified by educators in a manner that made it more suitable for classroom practice. Several behavioral variations, especially for learners with special needs, are in education practice today.

Educators in the early 1900s were not aware of pedagogical problems in U.S. schools until John Dewey, education philosopher and professor at the University of Chicago, started writing and speaking out on the shortcomings of school environments. Educators who worked to implement Dewey's philosophy as principles of pedagogy joined a movement labeled *progressive education.*

In the 1950s, during the years of the behavioristic influence on education and psychology in the United States, a variety of books based on behavioristic theories were published for teachers. Following the trend of modeling theories from other disciplines, authors of these publications based their recommended classroom disciplinary practices on theories described in the works of psychologists like Watson (1878–1958), Guthrie (1886–1959), and Thorndike (1874–1949). About the same time, *Gestaltism* had a major influence on psychology and education in Europe. Behaviorism and Gestaltism took a similar stance, in that both theorized a modification of behavior through influences on sensory attention.

In the 1950s, while psychology in the United States was still influenced predominantly by behaviorism, a variation labeled *operant conditioning* was introduced by psychologist B. F. Skinner (1904–1990). Skinner, however, objected to the classification of his work as theoretical. In his view, he narrowly described observations during controlled studies with no intent to establish *principals of behavior* from what was recorded. Skinner described his work as a focus on human factors that could be directly manipulated on the one hand, and, on the other hand human factors not manipulated by the experimenter but thought to be influenced by factors that could be directly manipulated.

Following a long period under the influence of behaviorism, the fields of psychology and education turned to interests in *humanistic studies*. Some in the field referred to this new category as *affective studies*. By 1970, practices in education included several variations on the theme of *humanistic education* and *humanistic psychology*. Today, in the year 2003, some universities still maintain departments of humanistic psychology. There are also active scholarly journals, such as *The Humanistic Psychologist*, the *Journal of Humanistic Psychology*, and the *Journal of Phenomenological Psychology*, that currently publish learned works in the field.

Early in the 1970s, psychologist Albert Ellis introduced what he termed *rational-emotive therapy* (RET), primarily as a humanistic/affective approach for resolving psychological problems commonly found among children. Soon thereafter, practices that utilized aspects of RET appeared in child psychology practices and grade-school classrooms. As was common with earlier trends, studies in education turned to psychology for theory supportive of humanistic/affective foundations. Here, educators discovered theoretical and philosophical foundations for these new approaches in *existentialism* and *phenomenology*. Education explored these concepts through the philosophical works of Georg Friedrich Hegel (1770–1831), Immanuel Kant (1724–1804), Edmund Husserl (1859–1938), and William James (1842–1910). James devoted a substantial section of his two-volume book *Principles of Psychology* to consciousness of the self.

Humanistic educators in the 1970s soon realized that John Dewey's thinking in the early 1900s had been influenced by Hegel, Kant, Husserl, and James. As a result, in the 1970s, Dewey's works were once again being studied, but now in the context of phenomenology and existentialism.

In 1978, specializing in the foundations of education, philosopher Maxine Greene bridged the gap between existentialism, phenomenology, and the practice of teaching in a series of essays. Greene's exceptional work brought clarity to *studies of the person* (children and teachers) for scholars and students in educational foundations. Also in the 1970s, along with educator interest in individuals as members of groups (classroom, school, family, community, etc.), there was an increased awareness of the collaborative role of the school in family and community relations. Several major developments were primarily responsible for the emergence of this phenomenon at that time; two are noted here.

First was the emergence of federally funded educational programs like Head Start for low-income families. Here, in addition to preschool education for children of the poor, medical, nutritional, and social services were also federally funded.

Second, there was considerable social pressure from minority communities after a slow pace of school desegregation following the Supreme Court ruling of 1957. Today, almost fifty years later, political entanglements in cities and resistance from upper-income communities—among other pressures—have prevented full implementation of school desegregation.

Since the 1970s, Head Start program guidelines mandated parent involvement in policy matters affecting neighborhood programs. The implementation of Head Start and desegregation legislation helped established *parent involvement* as an essential feature of early schooling.

In urban communities, adults pressed for greater community control of their public schools; for a brief period of time, some urban communities achieved collaborative community control. At the same time, other districts settled for heightened home–school collaborations. Today, a form of school–community collaboration is in place, though it is considerably less than the original intent of national parent involvement or community control. All communities with Head Start, and schools with Title l financing, must have parent involvement programs in place prior to funding.

The education establishment gradually embraced home–school collaborations, and university scholars eventually looked to disciplines like *anthropology* and *sociology* to guide this new and important practice. Here, the academy found cultural and theoretical foundations reported in anthropological studies that were conducted in the 1940s and '50s by Ruth Benedict (1887–1948), Franz Boas (1858–1942), and Margaret Mead (1901–1978) as essential for studies in child/family/school collaborations in education.

Given the fact that information processing is fundamental to learning, it is rather remarkable that texts designed for educators seldom model fundamental aspects of cognitive neuroscience. We now know from work in several related fields that information is sent by the organism from an experience to the brain through the central nervous system (CNS). Other information sent by the body to itself is processed through the peripheral nervous system (PNS). Through the PNS, the brain tells the body to walk, reach, grasp, run, or get ready for a dangerous experience (fight or flee), just to name a few. This latter phenomenon (PNS) is only peripherally related to primary knowledge acquisition. The CNS and PNS are discussed in chapter 4 (Acquiring Knowledge) in greater detail.

Chapters in this book are organized to reflect the flow of information starting with human experience, followed by attention, perception, acquiring knowledge, memory, and finally, retrieval and performance. For many psychologists and neuroscientists, memory is the final stage in the chain because this represents what has been learned. For educators, the final stage is retrieval and performance because the evaluation of their students is, more often than not, based on paper-and-pencil performance.

As educators in the academy continue to examine the many challenges posed by public, private, and religious school systems, studies on information processing seem to remain the work of disciplines not fully explored by scholars in education.

Currently, studies in *cognitive psychology* and *cognitive neuroscience* that examine the processing of information through animal and human studies provide intriguing potentials. It is surprising that the nature and function of the neuron, the center of information processing in the human conceptual system, is rarely written about or discussed by education scholars.

Studies and active scholarship in these areas are in a timely position to inform modern classroom practices. The distance between scholarship and knowledge in the neurosciences and education practice is one of great magnitude. The bridging of this gap will require attention to *philosophy, theory,* and *practice* in both domains. The primary purpose of this book is to bridge the gap between these areas of scholarship.

Over the years, as educators have studied and researched influences in education practice, a number of philosophers and theorists continually surface in texts and conversations. In scholarly studies, these names—along with primary aspects of their theories—are generally known. This group includes, but is not limited to, John Dewey, Erik

Erikson, Sigmund Freud, Maxine Greene, J. McVicker Hunt, Maria Montessori, Elizabeth Peabody, Jean Piaget, Lev Vygotsky, B. F. Skinner, and James B. Watson, just to name a few.

Because of the reader's likely familiarity with these figures, when possible, this writing will integrate emerging research in cognitive neuroscience with the earlier works of these icons.

What is rather remarkable is that with the recent quantity and quality of work on learning that is being conducted from various perspectives of cognitive neuroscience, biology, psychology, and anthropology, educators have launched few cooperative endeavors to benefit from these new developments.

In an important work, John T. Bruer (1997) cautioned teachers about their preoccupation with implementing activities presumably designed to capture special capacities in the brain. Bruer cautioned that the entire education community was off in the wrong direction with its entrepreneurial zeal, and suggested that accuracy in education literature had not bridged the gap between neuroscience and the classroom to the extent that what is then known could be made useful. The work in this book endeavors to bridge that gap.

ONE

Experience

With an increasing number of memories, fresh paths of displacement are constantly coming into existence. For that reason it has
been found advantageous to follow out all the different perceptions
fully, so that the most favorable of all the paths may be discovered.
This is the task of cognitive thought, which thus emerges as a preparation for practical thought, though in fact it only developed out
of the latter at a late stage.

—Sigmund Freud

The word *experience* calls forth the notion of *participation*. The participant can be attending to an experience that pairs the interaction of a
participant with others through observing or performing in the experience. Scholars who are active in the study of experience have expanded
concepts of experience to include *thought* and *intention* (Greene 1978,
1988; Dreyfus and Hall 1982).

We have all heard that people, and certainly children, *learn by doing*.
This truism implies that participation in an experience can enhance cognitive benefits that might accrue. Participation can include observing
(attending) and being embroiled in the center of an activity (experience). This writing includes *thought* in the concept of experience (Holt
1976; Denton 1974). It is also true that the inclusion of thought in this
context does not receive common agreement among all scholars (Burnett 1988). Many consider thought essential to experience. Especially in
schooling, reflection and contemplation by students performing classroom tasks are emerging as significant aspects of teaching and learning
(Greene 1988).

From birth, neonates and infants seem driven to acquire as much information as possible about objects and events in their new environments. Experiences that lead them to discover small objects on the floor, tabletop, and elsewhere encourage them to put objects in their mouth for a taste test; the object might be shaken to determine if it will make a sound and, finally, it might be thrown to the floor just to see what happens. Investigations are conducted by creepers (pre-crawling stage), crawlers (pre-walking stage), and toddlers (standing stage) whenever they encounter objects.

During the neonatal period, before their first words, infants are acquiring communication skills. Experiences available to them during this period are attractive and inviting. Infants thrive as participants in experiences around them. They learn rather quickly that actions and events can lead to other actions and events that are often associated with the previous ones. Some of the consequences are pleasant and some are not. Infants also learn that there are protocols associated with human experiences; some are common etiquette and good manners, while others are related to the most efficient manner to gain knowledge of our environment and/or satisfy individual needs.

Infants also learn from experiences with caregivers and from caregiver reactions to their own behaviors that *taking turns* is an important way to communicate and expand experiences. Infants master this skill rather early; some have suggested that this interactive experience is innate (Chomsky 1976). It has been frequently observed that infants gaze into the eyes of caregivers while listening to noises, movements, words of the caregiver, and their own babbling; they take turns in conversations with the caregiver (Jaffe, Stern, and Perry 1973).

Childhood experiences that emerge from conversations become the basic format for later teaching and learning in classrooms, for the transmission of culture in family, and for engaging with the larger society beyond school, family, and neighborhood (Bronfenbrenner 1979).

Early stages in the life of infants are replete with experiences like observing the caregiver turning on the water faucet in the bathtub. The observing infant concludes from previous experience that a bath will happen, soon to be followed by warm cuddly pajamas, and sometime later to bed (sleep). The simple act of the caregiver turning on the water for bathing can excite the infant's recall (memory) of similar experiences with these events (movements, mannerisms) and objects (self in water in the bathtub to be followed by pajamas—bed—sleep).

THE SIGNIFICANCE OF EXPERIENCE IN DEVELOPMENTAL THEORY

Erikson, Piaget, Freud, Skinner, and Vygotsky are the most well known among theorists who have focused on childhood experience as basic to learning and development. They suggest that, in a variety of ways, knowledge acquisition is molded by experiences with peers, families, schools, and other social institutions. Each theorist, however, has a unique perspective on the manner in which learners acquire knowledge from their experiences.

By now, even the informed public is aware that Sigmund Freud's theories of development were influenced by the ways in which social institutions (family, school, society) and social experiences in general vary for individuals based on *gender*.

Attention to gender differences did not appear unusual during the time of Freud's major works, and these gender differences were taken for granted and framed in a superior/inferior biological paradigm. This Freudian framing had serious consequences for the manner in which social institutions assigned benefits and burdens based on gender.

As an adult, Freud studied his own childhood experiences with each of his parents and concluded that variations emerging from these experiences were grounded in gender. Though his work concentrated on gender identity, it was screened through the professional language of his day and labeled *sexual identity*. Some time later, Freud's theory was classified as *psychosexual*. Even today, it is common in popular media to refer to gender differences as *sexual differences*.

The social backdrop of Freud's work was framed during a period in history when females were severely limited in their participation in matters of social significance. After giving birth to children, women's lives were patterned by what males thought they should be—primarily child rearing and conducting domestic family affairs. The roles of childbearing and child rearing were often not performed by the same women.

Women in affluent families gave birth, but their infants were often the responsibility of women who worked as caregivers.

From the late 1800s through the 1960s, Freud's theories were taught in most of the universities and professional schools where psychoanalysts and other therapists associated with that field received their training.

Although Freud's work concentrated on human sexuality as the primary influence on experiences of human growth and development, the work of one of his most influential students, Erik Erikson theorized that societal experiences, molded with significant others, framed the primary influences in human development. Erikson's work has been framed as *psychosocial*.

The works of Freud, Erikson, Piaget, and Vygotsky tend to focus more on the influences of society on the individual, rather than individual influences on the environment. Here, the individual (self) is the primary shaping force that is influenced by social institutions and groups. From this perspective, the self in Freud's terms is the *ego*. Freud, Erikson, and Piaget (but excluding Vygotsky) can be grouped as stage theorists. They describe development and learning in steps and stages (Morgan 1999).

According to Freud, the power that drives an individual to create a significant social position leading to survival and existence rests in the *id*. The id seeks self-satisfaction without a concern for the needs of others; the ego, concerned with learned social values, serves to keep the id under control.

Though commonly stated in popular media, humans do not have instincts according to Freud. Beginning at birth, humans do have drives; from birth, humans are *driven* to create a place for themselves, and strive to survive. Individuals are therefore born with certain drives that are initially controlled by the id.

Chief among the early drives is the need of infants for physical support and stability in their new environment. Neonates and infants can be fearful of losing support and the inability to satisfy hunger.

Shortly after birth, if the adult holding the infant lowers his or her holding posture quickly, the infant will gasp in fear of losing support, and often cry. Anything touching the infant's mouth, or parts of the face near the mouth, will initiate a sucking motion with the lips. Seeking support and food are two basic drives. Freud theorized the id as the psychological impetus motivating the human drive for existence.

What Freud described as id and ego were accepted, with some modifications, by the other developmentalists Erikson, Piaget, and Vygotsky.

Drives have various properties to which Freud attributed innate sexuality. Among them is the sucking of the lips and mouth to acquire food during infancy. This drive will find its sexual expression later as, for example, in the use of the lips for various acts such as kissing to express love and affection. Psychoanalysts discuss with patients the need for placing things in the mouth—nail biting, biting the ends of a pencil (between writing thoughts), dedication to smoking cigarettes, and holding a pipe in one's mouth, though seldom lit, for example.

Erikson viewed Freud as too preoccupied with sexuality (gender) and he focused on the fulfillment of psychological needs. Erikson theorized that neonates and infants during their first year of life were driven to *confirm* that their new environment could be *trusted* to satisfy their needs. Erikson called this period of development *basic trust/mistrust.*

Of all the gradual learning experiences from infancy to adolescence, maturation of language learning can be tracked with the greatest accuracy. Despite the complexity of the grammatical structures experienced from adult speech, most children under the age of twelve months have had enough experiences through social interaction to enable them to make distinctions among speech sounds and accomplish a vocabulary of fifty or more words (Lenneberg 1967).

Vygotsky's theory describes human development primarily through the social experiences of language interaction. In his view, language experience is primarily responsible for development and learning.

Like Piaget, Vygotsky's theory focuses on cognitive development. Piaget (1970) agreed that language is an element in cognitive development; language, however, requires *thought* and therefore occurs later in the child's life. Here, Piaget applied Freud's concept of ego as the theoretical framing for the *self.* According to Piaget, the child's thought, although lacking maturity, is focused primarily on the self (ego). Before the age of twelve months, children have too little awareness of the properties of objects outside of the self through which to interpret their own daily experiences and how these experiences are related to others.

From his observations of the language of childhood, Vygotsky labeled *egocentric speech* (as defined by Piaget) as *private speech* (thought) of young children. Vygotsky (1934) theorized that speech is first influenced by language experiences initiated by caregivers. Next, the behavior of children is influenced by speech directed toward them individually—*social speech.* Children use private speech in conversations with themselves.

Finally, children are able to use their own speech to influence the actions of others. These phases of speech development, according to Vygotsky, are influenced by language experiences with peers, family, and more mature speakers.

B. F. Skinner's work on language acquisition departs from most popular views of his time. Skinner suggests that children learn the language of their country in a language-rich family environment. Skinner suggests that, as children develop, their first words are learned from imitating others in their environment. Experiences in family require communication. The young must achieve language competence to communicate needs and desires and to participate in family experiences.

The further along children become in development, the stronger their desire to participate in experiences of the family becomes. According to Skinner, children become language competent through imitating other language-competent people.

For example, an eighteen-month-old child might make a request of a parent, "Want water." The parent opens the refrigerator and takes out the water bottle and starts to pour some into a glass. The child responds with, "No, want water." The parent opens the refrigerator door and returns the water when suddenly the child points to the juice container and repeats, "Want water." The parent replies, "Ok, but that is juice, not water." From this experience, the child has expanded her vocabulary by adding a new word, learned when to use it, and learned that all liquid drinks are not called "water." Skinner theorized that *reinforcement* and *shaping* (to be discussed later) were essential elements in learning language, as well as most other things (1957).

John B. Watson (1878–1958) and B. F. Skinner (1904–1990) were psychologists who took a sharp departure from the theories of developmentalists like Freud, Piaget, Erikson, and Vygotsky. Expanding the work of Ivan Pavlov, the originator of *classical conditioning*, Skinner and

Watson became psychology's most famous supporters of what has become known as *behaviorism.*

Ivan Petrovich Pavlov (1849–1936), disdainful of the new field of psychology, received the Nobel Prize in 1904 for his research on the human digestive system. It was during his work with animals that he discovered their salivating reaction when a bell was sounded to note their feeding time. The dogs' salivating was stimulated by the sound of the bell because, for them, feeding experiences always followed the bell sound. Pavlov's work had a significant influence on Watson. After completing graduate studies at the University of Chicago, Watson was appointed professor of research at Johns Hopkins University.

Watson was most influential in the field of psychology during the 1930s and '40s. Watson's theory rested on the simple notion that child development and learning were influenced primarily through experiences with caregivers, and heredity had no or only minimal influence. He suggested that children have no desire to repeat experiences for which they were punished or ignored but that children desire to repeat experiences from which they gain pleasure or for which they are rewarded. This reward could be in the form of words of approval or praise. His work was generally too narrow for the research community, whose greater interest turned to Skinner. Watson fell out of favor with the scholarly community because of questionable tactics employed in studies with children. (Today, practically all research activity must be reviewed and approved by committees formed in institutions where the major researcher is employed.)

This *Institutional Review Board* (IRB) was formed as the result of heinous experimental activities in Nazi Germany and the United States. The Nazi experimentation on homosexuals, gypsies, and people of Jewish descent is now well known. Tuskegee experiments conducted by the U.S. government are less well known. Here, medication was withheld from African American males who were diagnosed with syphilis but who were told that they were being treated so that medical science could study the effects.

After being influenced by studying Watson's work, Skinner presented a more complex version of Pavlov's classical conditioning while, at the same time, folding into his ideas a more refined description of Watson's theories. Skinner redefined Freud's id and ego concepts as basic to human experiences. In the Skinner model of human development, drives that are observed in human experiences can be included within the framework of what are actually *operants*. In this regard, Skinner suggested that observations of human experiences revealed how individuals *operated* on their environment. Skinner theorized that *consequences* resulting from human experiences led to individual control of these operants.

To manipulate or control behavior, Skinner suggested that consequences resulting from pleasurable experiences would result in a desire by the participant to repeat the behavior. Those who wished behaviors of others to be repeated—a teacher, for example—could provide reinforcement to ensure the repetition of desired behavior. Experiences from which learners do not derive pleasure are weakened, with little desire for repetition. This concept of Skinnerian control and shaping of behavior has become known as the principal of *operant conditioning*.

Operant conditioning theory and Skinner's work with humans and animals toward a refinement of reinforcement strategies are reflected in various methods of classroom management today to eliminate or reshape what have been labeled "behavior problems." There are also many other planned classroom experiences that involve techniques of *shaping* similar to those first developed by Skinner (1957).

Classroom Experiences

Many experiences occurring in classrooms are planned by teachers and based upon what educators think learners at a particular age or school grade should be taught. There are other experiences occurring in classrooms that are initiated through student interaction. Some of these experiences are neither planned nor intended.

Learners engage in many out-of-school experiences, and learning obviously occurs in these environments as well. In fact, some learners tend to have knowledge and skills available to them in some environments that are not necessarily available to them in others.

Sometimes, children who appear somewhat withdrawn and quiet during classroom experiences can be found in other environments, such as the schoolyard, organizing and leading other children in play and demonstrating socially interactive leadership qualities.

Teachers are also surprised when students in the same classroom, receiving practically the same lesson content and generally sharing the same environment, score substantially different on tests designed to measure what has been learned. Under such circumstances, the common environment in which learners are exposed to similar experiences is certainly an important factor.

An equally important factor in any commonly shared experience, whether in the classroom or away from school activities, is the extent to which the learner's attention is attracted to the unfolding elements of an experience.

Today's teachers are somewhat aware of the value of gaining the learner's attention. Experienced teachers often include an *attention getter* at the front end of their lesson but give little thought to the fundamental structure guiding this act. How experiences are attended to, filtered, and processed by perception for memory storage is influenced by the learner's values, motivation, emotional state, health status, and related variables. The engagement of the learner in a planned experience can also be influenced by the manner in which the experience unfolds and persists (Treisman 1960; Pashler 1998).

Variations emerging from experiences also enact a role in the structuring of a context. *Context* refers to the relationship between the learner and the experience. Context can have a positive influence; it can contribute to reasons the learner might ignore parts or the entirety of an experience. Acquiring knowledge from experiences varies among individuals because, in part, individuals carry memory traces of different interpretations of previous experiences. A learner's mental state assists in organizing information from new experiences, and that helps frame images of the here-and-now world.

Two Children: Interrelated Experiences

One morning, just before leaving for school, Tara, a twelve-year-old African American girl, is having a bowl of cereal with her mother. She casually asks, "Why is the president always white?" Her mother stalls before answering and a great deal goes through her mind. She doesn't want her daughter, an honor student in a predominantly white school, to be burdened with the negative racial attitudes that, in her view, are prevalent in her country. She thinks silently while pondering a response, knowing that there are things over which no one has control and that her bright twelve-year-old might not fully understand. She stalls for time, "We must hurry for school. Your father and I will discuss that question with you after dinner tonight."

In another part of town, Michael, a white eighth grader, while having breakfast with his father, asks, "Dad, why are all the NBA players African American?" Michael's father pauses because he does not want his son to be resentful of persons identified as members of racial groups that are different from his own. He is trying to think of ways to explain that being a good athlete takes hard work and, regardless of color, any person could make it to the NBA if that was his most important career goal.

He is cautious because his son might detect avoidance in his response. He names the few white NBA players with whom his son is familiar and says, "What about *those* white guys?"

Tara and Michael are making meaning from their experiences in different environments. The new meaning they are making is becoming integrated with previously acquired knowledge. This process starts at an early age, and the meanings that children make provides a backdrop to their development as they become fully capable, by approximately nine years of age, of experiencing and expressing emotion. Often, new knowledge does not call for immediate responses but sometimes it does, and children act upon what they believe at that given time.

Her parents never told Tara that she could not be best friends with Michael, but her experiences tell her that her family attends a church where the minister and others are African American. She has also observed a change in speaking patterns and vocabulary when her parents converse with African American friends, and these nuances are not present when they speak to whites, who are seldom in their home.

For Tara, such experiences might evoke emotions that signal the need for additional information from African American adults before acting upon her emotional attraction to Michael. It is rather likely that Michael is similarly using white adults to examine his emotions concerning the same emotional terrain.

Not all childhood experiences occur in the protected environments of home around the breakfast table. For most children, classrooms, playgrounds, soccer fields, basketball courts, interactions within their friendship groups, and their after-school ballet classes provide significant social venues.

During such activities, children create friendships with teachers, coaches, and significant others; in later grades, they contemplate mate choices. As they reach out for relationships, social attractions are framed by their acting on emotional values that emerge from conative experiences.

EXPERIENCE: THEORY OF CONTEXT AND CONTENT

Context and content of an experience are central to concepts elaborated by Albert Bandura. He theorized that, early in the lives of children, their experiences in family, where they observe the performance of other family members, ensure learning through observing. This approach has been called *observational learning.*

Borrowing somewhat from the work of Skinner, Bandura (1986) suggested that children select certain behaviors from experiences and tend to repeat experiences from which they derive rewards. For example, following a family experience where a parent reads a storybook to children, a child from the group that is later observed reading the book for pleasure will be drawn to reading in the future because the parent initially read to children, and later praised the child upon noticing him in the act of reading. Because the child was attracted to reading through an experience with others, and reinforced by a significant adult, Bandura's theory was called *social learning theory.* Bandura's theories that describe a social context for child growth and development have been used as a scientific basis to support programs that encourage parents and other caregivers to aid in the work of the school by reading to their children.

Bandura's views concerning children's thinking have been integrated with cognitive concepts and can be associated with those of Piaget and Erikson. The influence of social experiences on cognitive development and imitative behavior during childhood has been refined by Bandura and others (Mischel 1973), and is now referred to as *social cognitive theory*.

Children and other family members are often alarmed to meet their classroom teacher in a neighborhood grocery store or other common community facility. Many do not conceptualize that out-of-school experiences are a natural part of the teacher's life, just as they are with other families. Classifying the teaching and learning experience calls forth various perspectives that, in part, are influenced by the experience. Often, parents want to know that their child has the best teacher in their child's school. Parents have experienced schooling during their own childhood; as adults, they might blame (or praise) their perception of their school experience for their own failure or success as adults. They might vow not to allow their children to repeat their school experience or they can accept responsibility for not doing well and support the work of their current school.

Every adult has had a variety of teachers during his or her lifetime. These earlier experiences have helped to establish a unique view of schooling and education. It is also true that contributors to major achievements in U.S. society, like inventors of new medicines, explorers, and astronauts, at some time in their life, were in kindergarten and the first grade. Everyone has had a "schooling" experience that (in part) helped shape his or her ideas and behaviors to accept and support the social rules of society.

The responsibility invested in teachers to shape the classroom experiences of children, and pass each child on to the next level in his or her growth and development, is a daunting task for many. It is a social responsibility requiring a period of training and education, replete with self-doubt and frequent self-evaluation.

The responsibility, self-doubt, and self-assessment are a part of the mystique that can attract people to the profession of teaching.

The schooling environment in the United States can be viewed as a major challenge for our capitalist system. Problems in U.S. public education are created by extreme differences in family income, and can be deemed systemic. For example, and consistently at a minimum, 20 percent of all children in the United States grow up in families and neighborhoods of poverty. That percentage has fluctuated between 20 and 25 percent since 1950 (Wright 1995; Farley and Allen 1987).

This is cited here because school-age children growing up in the United States will more than likely enter adulthood using a language dialect common to their family and neighborhood, and the language dialect of the poor is different from the language dialect regarded as standard for adults (Bailey and Thomas 1998). Language and communication are basic to all human experiences. In the marketplace, one is valued through one's language competence, and the languages of low-income families are more than likely negatively valued.

Despite the fact that Atlanta, Charlotte, and Birmingham are major metropolitan cities in the South, for example, a Southern dialect cannot be detected by listening to TV newscasters who have grown up in these Southern cities. The language and speech patterns found on newscasts throughout the South are much like those in other parts of the country. Media have selected a standard for language, and special schools have been established to teach this style. Influences of regional dialect have been eliminated.

When we are discussing behaviors and styles of articulation, it can be equally important that we acknowledge that children's styles are being observed and valued by teachers and significant others. Behaviors and styles can be found in written expressions to an assignment, an oral response in a dramatic performance, or casual conversation. Audiences can include siblings, peers, parents, teachers, and other knowledgeable observers. Persons in the audience who are valuing an individual's performance bring to that task a set of their own values. Depending on their position and power in society, their values could change the direction of one's life. Perpetuating the values of one's community can be problematic when such values are nonstandard.

For example, highly paid athletes can use neighborhood speech patterns (dialects) different from commonly respected standards and remain popular and valued, as long as they are athletes. Only athletes who achieve standard speech patterns will become sports announcers, and some do. Dialects that are identified with the poor, regardless of race or religion, gain common respect in their neighborhood of origin but only occasionally and under very narrow social conditions in standard environments.

Because she is the wife of the president, the social status of Laura Bush does not change when she says *wadn't* in the place of *wasn't*.

Hadn't is also common to the dialect of the South. It is not unusual for individuals to have several dialects that can be switched as their audience changes. There may be a style one uses when at home relaxed with family and a different style when, for example, one is speaking to colleagues or to customers in the workplace.

Occasionally, a less-formal style is used when one is with friendship or racial groups. Under such circumstances, social acquaintances might allow a nonstandard word or phrase to appear at the wrong time. Often, an adult in the home assumes the role of correcting language usage by children during conversations or by shaping word choices and pronunciations.

These examples are discussed in the context of experience because speakers are unable to participate in, or fully benefit from, experiences when they are denied a presence because of their dialect or their lack of comprehension. Other persons might avoid, or modify interacting with, those who cannot use Standard English.

> No topic in modern sociolinguistics has engendered more interest than African American Vernacular English. Furthermore, this interest has not been restricted to the sociolinguistic research community. As evidenced by sporadic national controversies that have played out in media over the past several decades, the public at large has also been captivated by the sociopolitical and educational implications attended to this language variety. (Wolfram and Thomas 2002, preface)

Society has dealt with African American language variation in various ways. In popular media, it is often a target for humorous ridicule and entertainment. Even black parents who are relentless about shaping language experiences for their own children can themselves be attracted to viewing programming where variations on African American vernacular English (AAVE) are integrated by African American performers.

Since the end of slavery, after which efforts toward public education for all children in the United States gradually became a reality, the most common African American dialect has had many name changes. This has established a basis for the high level of interest that continues to grow in general society.

Starting with *Negro Dialect,* it has at different times been progressively labeled *Substandard Negro English, Nonstandard Negro English, Black English, Vernacular Black English/Black English Vernacular, Afro-American English, Ebonics, African American Vernacular English, African American Language,* and *Spoken Soul* (Wolfram and Thomas 2002).

Responses from the academic community of grade schools, colleges and universities, and the workplace remain mixed. Because of various structural realities, it is not unexpected that these different treatments will continue.

In large school districts like Atlanta, Philadelphia, and parts of California, African American adults who speak African American Vernacular English (AAVE) are often employed as classroom teachers, thus perpetuating a modeling, for good or not so good.

For good, because of what has been noted: there is a thriving entertainment market for such speakers. For not so good: outside of the entertainment media, there are too few attractive choices for speakers of AAVE to be accepted at all levels of integrated regional language experiences. In part, this is because of the persistence among African Americans to duplicate common linguistic experiences within their groups.

Linguistic scholars report that although white immigrants who are recent arrivals in urban centers gradually adjust to new grammatical experiences of regional and urban sounds in the United States, this is not the case for Native Americans, Hispanics, and African Americans.

So far, the sound changes sweeping across the United States have been portrayed as if they were general phenomena affecting to varying degrees all levels of the speech community. But this is not so. In Boston, New York, Philadelphia, Detroit, Cleveland, Chicago, San Francisco, and Los Angeles, the progress of the sound changes we have been studying stop short of the racial line. All speakers who are socially defined as white, mainstream, or Euro-American are involved in the changes to one degree or another. There are leaders, and there are followers, but in the mainstream community it is almost impossible to find someone who stands completely apart. But for those children who are integral members of a sub-community that American society defines as "non-white"—black, Hispanic or Native American—the result is quite different. No matter how frequently they are exposed to the local vernacular, the new patterns of regional sound change do not surface in their speech. On the deeper level of syntax and semantics, the African American community is carried even further away on a separate current of grammatical change, and a very sizable fraction of the Hispanic community is being carried along with them. (Labov 2001, 506)

Imagine a teacher providing planned experiences in a class for a group of twenty-five children. Some will receive information not completely available to others because of subtle (and sometimes major) differences between syntax, semantics, and oral phrasing heard in the family and what is commonly heard during classroom experiences.

It was not uncommon for immigrant groups in the late 1800s and early 1900s to have difficulty in schools for some of the same reasons. For them, adults in the home spoke their language of origin, which was unlike the language of the classroom. Jacob Riis and Jane Addams, through the Settlement House movement, established programs in neighborhood centers to provide relief in light of such problems (Morgan 1999).

For these same groups, new approaches to classroom experiences, first developed by Johann Pestalozzi (1746–1827), were finding their way into experimental schools being tried by transcendentalists. Amos Bronson Alcott (1799–1888) opened the Temple School in 1825 and hired Elizabeth Peabody, founder of the U.S. kindergarten movement, as its first teacher. Here, language interaction provided the foundation for learning experiences. In the midst of this revolutionary idea of adults actually giving attention to children, Peabody recorded some of these earlier experiences.

> About twenty children came the first day. They were all under ten years of age, excepting two or three girls. I became his assistant to teach Latin, to such as might desire to learn. Mr. Alcott sat behind his table, and the children were placed in chairs so far apart, that they could easily touch each other. He then asked one separately, what idea she or he had of the object of coming to school. To learn; was the first answer. To learn what? By pursuing this question, all the common exercises of school were brought up—successfully—even philosophy. (Cohen and Scheer 1997, 73)

Testing in schools has been nationalized for the most part, and children in most classrooms are measured with standardized tests. Leaders in education have determined that information should be standardized in the manner that TV speech has been. Being in attendance during a classroom experience, however, does not mean that all children within the purview of an experience have equal opportunities to benefit from such experiences. Differences between family experiences due to income and other disparities also mean that inequalities exist after children return home from school.

In *Meaningful Differences in the Everyday Experience of Young American Children,* Hart and Risley (1995) described their study of forty-two children ages six to thirty-six months. Children were selected from families in three socioeconomic ranges: professional income, middle-class income, and welfare income. For sixty months, each child was observed during language experiences in their home for one hour a week. The observer recorded children's language by detailing each of their attempts at language interaction with the caregiver. The caregiver's responses were recorded as *interrogative, declarative, directive, positive,* and/or *negative.* The study reported significant differences between language experiences in welfare homes and similar experiences in middle-income and affluent homes. The study concluded by strongly supporting remedial language development experiences in schools. Schools populated mostly by African American and Hispanic children were least likely to provide programs beyond the basics.

Studies have suggested in-group differences that might be determined primarily by income. In a study of black children from three different social classes, Bardouille-Crema (1986) reported that the high socioeconomic status (SES) group scored higher on reasoning, and the concept of sequence, classification, and causation than did the lower SES groups. This could be a function of family life, schooling, or teacher quality.

THE GENERIC SHAPING OF EXPERIENCE

In addition to the classical shaping of behavior by teachers and psychologists, there is a persistent generic shaping of public experiences through the type and content of information disseminated in schools, libraries, and divisions of our government, just to name a few. This shaping is designed in part to maintain a controllable national social-class structure that teachers and their students will support (Apple 1979).

Historically, too few students and teachers have had the freedom or inclination to confront this persistent shaping of school experiences to match a prevailing national agenda (Henry 1965).

The shaping of school and public experiences is more often than not perpetuated through the framing of language. For example, the phrase *minorities and women* is commonly found in various media. This shaping of a common racial experience in U.S. society prefers to ignore gender differences within minority groups, thus creating two groups: minority men and minority women as one group, and white women as the other.

This framing provides political cleavage between white women and minority women by placing them in separate groups and thereby *reducing the power of all women*. In reality, the two groups should be noted as minority males in one group, and women in the other group. After all, black women are also women. This modest change of describing the groups as *minority males and women* could pose a major threat to those in power who benefit from dissension between minority women and white women.

One of the more prevalent acts of shaping public experience in the United States seems to have almost complete national support. Seldom are our schoolchildren taught that the country in which they live is the *United States*, not *America*. America is not a country; it is a continent. It would require a lot of documentation to become a citizen of America. It would require citizenship in South America, Central America, Mexico, and Canada. However, one can be an American citizen, as are persons born in Mexico, Brazil, Canada, or Costa Rica, for example. It is also reasonable for citizens of North America, Central America, or South America to describe themselves as American.

A view of a world map would reveal that the landmass of South America is greater than that of the United States. Maps manufactured in the United States, however, often depict the United States as *larger* than South America.

EXPERIENCE AND ENVIRONMENT

Child development theorists have historically paired individual biological systems with environmental systems in explaining the emergence of the whole child. The individual contributions of biology and experience to the developing child have also framed the basis for nature/nurture arguments. With intelligence at its core, some have argued that intelligence can undergo only minor changes from the influences of experience. They also suggest that individual intellectual potentials are predetermined by the biology of one's parents.

There are others who explain that the contribution of biology and experience to the establishment of intelligence is an incompatible framing for the argument. This group of scholars suggests that the discussion should be concerned with the relationship between biology and experience (how they interact) rather than a specific percentage that each might contribute to total intellectual capacity.

Urie Bronfenbrenner (1993) proposed a much larger role for experience. *Ecological systems theory* explains child development occurring within a complex system of experiences influenced at various levels of the environment. Bronfenbrenner proposed that experiences are not uniform in manner but represent a child's world of dynamic experiences. Varying with the age of the child, experiences occur in different contexts that include a microsystem, mesosystem, ecosystem, and macrosystem, each layer having an essential impact on the child's development (Bronfenbrenner 1993).

The *microsystem* includes experiences in the child's family and immediate surroundings. Here, experiences that involve parents and children interactively provide the foundation for child development. Prior to Bronfenbrenner's work, parental influences *on* children were emphasized, rather than reciprocal experiences.

Bronfenbrenner described the next layer of experience as the *meso system.* This layer starts with interconnecting the microsystems of home, neighborhood, school, day-care center, and other community events that foster childhood experiences. Here, children start to witness the family supporting the work of the school. Links between home, school, and community are established (Grolnick and Slowiaczek 1994).

The *ecosystem* includes experiences that do not necessarily involve children directly. Experiences here are created by institutions like social and welfare services, settlement houses, and community centers, where activities are planned to provide experiences like social networks and exchanges of information for adults.

The *macrosystems* form the outermost experiential ring and involve experiences of families within local values, national custom, law, and other social mores.

Family experiences with events like marriage, divorce, adoptions, and birth can entangle family members in religious customs, child custody laws, financial responsibilities, and residential needs.

As humans, experience is all that we have. Experience was also the foundation for Darwin's observations that all humans have survived from the same ancestors. Throughout human existence, a process of natural selection has created variants that ensure the survival of some species and not others; survival is significantly influenced by the manner in which groups interact with their experience (Gould 1977).

Experience is basic to our neural networking because our central nervous system (the spinal cord and the brain) has no access to the outside world where experiences unfold, except through our central and peripheral nervous systems.

> The effects of experience on the functional conductivity of neural pathways are reflected in morphological change, which depends upon the degree of activity and synchrony in the inputs converging on common targets. Morphological change seems to be triggered most effectively by synchronous input, and it results in more effective synaptic connections for the active inputs and less effective connections for the inactive ones. (Squire 1987, 32)

Two

Attention

> I used to be scared of him all the time, he tanned me so much. I reckoned I was scared now, too; but in a minute I see I was mistaken—that is, after the first jolt, as you might say, when my breath sort of hitched, he being so unexpected; but right away after I see I warn't scared of him worth bothering about. He was most fifty, and looked it. His hair was long and tangeled and greasy, and hung down, and you could see his eyes shining through like he was behind vines. It was all black, no gray; so was his long mixed up whiskers. There warn't no color in his face, where his face showed; it was white; not like another man's white, but a white to make a body sick, a white to make a body's flesh crawl—the toad white, a fish belly white.
>
> —*The Adventures of Huckleberry Finn*, Mark Twain

Scholars and psychologists were drawn to *attention* as a significant area of human behavior as early as the late 1800s. Sigmund Freud, during his little-known theorizing about neurons, became trapped in his *Project for a Scientific Psychology*. This was an absorbing task that his closest colleague, Wilhelm Fliess, insisted he should abandon.

During this time, Freud was writing about *neurons, axons,* and *dendrites* as sensory transmitters of sensations to the brain. Among other things, he could not explain how transmitted sensations could travel along a "track" from their point of origin to the brain while at the same time remaining available to simultaneous drives like hunger and sex. These were drives from which the human organism could not free itself.

Freud was searching for an internal objective entity that could be identified as attention. In one of the many letters to Fliess, Freud elicited Fliess' assistance in explaining the complex problem of a compromise made by individuals who must select among several simultaneously competing ideas for their singular attention: "Thus, as in the other neurosis, it is the result of compromise; but this compromise is not manifested in a substitution based on similarity of subject matter but in the displacement of attention along a series of ideas that are connected by having occurred simultaneously" (Freud 1954, 155).

Psychologist William James cited the same interest in 1890 when he framed his query in terms of the number of independent ideas to which an individual can attend to at once.

> The point seems to be that the number of things we can do depends on the difficulty of each task. A well-learned task, such as walking, takes little effort and does not impede us in the performance of another. A more difficult task such as walking along a high, narrow ledge requires more concentration and may impede our efforts to hold a conversation.
>
> Given that the number of things to which we can attend at once is very limited, what is our perception of events to which we are not attending? The act of switching our attention to an event may both blur our perception of that event and cause confusion in our judgments of its temporal properties. These are the critical observations for the experimental investigation of attention, and they suggest a method of study. If attention is the result of a serial device, should there not be difficulty in determining the details and time sequence of events that occur during the absence of our attention? (James 1890, 409)

In the 1950s, psychologist E. Colin Cherry studied selective attention as the "Cocktail Party Problem." Cherry conducted several studies in the MIT Research Laboratory of Electronics. His basic idea suggested that selective attention could be framed along the idea of groups of people simultaneously involved in conversations in a crowded room at a cocktail party. With this general context in mind, Cherry selected two groups for one of his studies (1953).

For one group study, two different spoken messages were presented simultaneously to both ears. In the second group, one spoken message was delivered to the right ear and a different message to the left ear.

The "cocktail party" concept becomes relevant in this experiment when one considers that complete words must be perceived during a "party" experience in which voices come from many different directions, and vary in pitch and articulation, as well as in accents and voice dynamics, just to name a few variables. Cherry reported that, as humans engage in conversations that are in a competing context, listeners use all of these variations to recognize speakers.

Among the early theoretical responses to Cherry's explanations of attention, Broadbent (1958) suggested that an internal mechanism served to filter out irrelevant information, because selection was made by the human system based on physical characteristics. Treisman's work on attention reported that attention was not influenced solely by physical characteristics but that the human system processes attention selectively through a persistent analysis of incoming sensations from all sources, followed by a rejection of what is considered irrelevant (1977). After Deutsch and Deutsch (1963) modified this explanation, it became known as the *filter-amplitude theory.*

The Broadbent (1958) explanation described a process that analyzed incoming sensations one after another, and following inputs could not be processed until the first one was complete. On the other hand, Deutsch and Deutsch as well as Treisman explained that the human organism could analyze a steady stream of sensations from which selections could be made. This "analysis of a number of simultaneously competing sensations" was what confounded Freud in his search for a scientific theory of psychology.

Kahneman's work was reported ten years later, and maybe the answer can be found there (1973). Kahneman explained that human attention systems were capable of dividing the *selection process* (divided attention); prior to processing, the processing network is influenced by competing sensations (Kahneman 1973). Kahneman's explanation, although supported by many, contradicted the work of others up to that time.

During the 1960s and '70s, philosophers and psychologists maintained a high level of interest in attention. Although each group spread the discussion in different directions, the fundamentals are surprisingly similar. In the 1960s, philosopher Alan White (1964) described objective and subjective concepts of attention for psychology and philosophy.

Some psychologists and philosophers have discussed paying attention in the context of a "set" or "frame of mind." Other psychologists speak of it

as a conative process or give it a selectivity role, and traditional philosophers have regarded it as a kind of internal watching or contemplating.
Let us look at its logical characteristics.

"Attending" sometimes means no more than being physically present, as
when we attend a lecture; sometimes it means being physically present
and looking after, as when a doctor attends to a wounded man or a porter
attends to our luggage. Sometimes it means being present and paying attention to something, as when we dance attendance on someone. It also
means paying attention to something irrespective of physical presence; it
is to be occupied with it in any of a variety of ways. It is this notion of
paying attention . . . though much of what I say is applicable to attending
of any kind. (White 1964, 4)

Although such European psychologists as Wilhelm Wundt (1832–
1920) approached the study of attention from a perspective of *sensory
processing*, James, who has been credited with providing psychology
with a comprehensive treatment of attention, suggested that individuals
were selective of experiences that were permitted to enter their sense
of consciousness (Norman 1976; Neisser 1982).

Probably no psychologist has written more than Wilhelm Wundt on
topics associated with experimental psychology, higher mental processes, and social behavior. Wundt had a significant influence on psychology in the United States because a considerable number of scholars
from the United States studied in his German laboratory of scientific
psychology, founded in Leipzig in 1879. Many consider him the founder
of modern psychology. He is also credited with establishing psychology
as a science—a search that Freud commenced, but failed to fulfill.

The son of a Lutheran minister, Wundt received a medical degree at
age twenty-four and went on to become an instructor in physiology. He
was a professor of philosophy in Zurich for one year and a member of
the faculty of medicine at Heidelberg University for seventeen years.
The first edition of his textbook on psychology was published in three
volumes of more than 550 pages each.

Wundt's influence became widespread among scholars from various
countries after they studied with him in his scientific laboratory in Leipzig. Upon returning to their home countries, they frequently engaged
in scientific studies of principles based on psychology as a science, and

the separation of philosophy and psychology. Wundt's concepts concerning attention also became the general view among psychologists in Germany at that time.

In studies concerning individual differences as indicated by what one decides to attend, German psychologists conceptualized these differences as errors rather than conscious intention or subconscious variation. In attention studies, this view posed a problem for many German psychologists in the testing movement, because these differences could not be eliminated, nor could they be scientifically accounted for (Goodenough 1949).

Gradually, psychologists in other countries (including the United States) who had been scholars in Wundt's lab started to publish their work and were able to define their particular domains of interest. Wundt's followers in the United States started to drift away from his experimental work on sensation, consciousness, feelings, and perceiving.

In North America, Wundt's link between learning and *thought* was replaced by animal and human studies designed to establish a link between learning and *behavior*. The early 1900s witnessed the rise of *behaviorism* as a major movement in psychology. Psychologists in the United States, under the influence of John B. Watson, became unaccepting of higher-level thinking that could not be empirically connected to observed behavior.

A surge of reports from psychologists in the 1960s and '70s also provided educators with ample staging points from which to launch their own studies of attention, first begun during Wundt's greatest influence.

Within the recent past, interest has returned to Wundt's early laboratory experiments. That interest has paired investigations of mood, emotions, and learning with memory (Byrnes 2001; Eysenck and Byrne 1994; Oakhill 1984).

All categories of consciousness, such as perception, attention, short-term memory, and long-term memory, were viewed simply as memory, which gradually emerged as a single concept of memory. In this view, short-term memory (STM) and long-term memory (LTM) are different stages, but still closely integrated with memory. Attention is considered by some to be a brief version of short-term memory.

In the 1990s, Baddeley found the need to restate the notion that "it is not one system but many. The systems range in storage duration from fractions of a second up to a lifetime, and in storage capacity from tiny buffer stores to long-term memory stores to the long-term memory system" (1998, 3).

Other studies avoided these divisions and focused on the process. Treisman (1969) reported that an experience to which the listener attends is processed for meaning. In the Treisman reports, aspects of the experience are excluded from processing by the system through filtering. Deutsch and Deutsch (1963) proposed an opposite view. They suggested that an entire experience is actually processed, even those aspects to which the perceiver does not attend. It was their view that selection occurs in the final memory processing stage, rather than filtering at the front end as proposed by Treisman.

Behaviors that imply that attention is being directed at a selected target are generally accepted by teachers as conclusive. Such common knowledge, however, can be deceptive. Children can be attending to an experience "in thought," in that the here-and-now classroom experience could have reminded the attending student of a previous event, and the student's attending can track in the direction of the new experience, serving to combine the new experience with the previous one, thus rendering an entirely new interpretation of the newly combined experiences.

Psychologists would identify the traces that remain as memory. In the absence of self-reporting, assessments of such traces cannot be accurately determined empirically. Our most up-to-date instruments that are designed to measure the capacity of individual memory rely upon self-reporting through a selected form of *performance*. The most common forms of performance designed to assess intellectual capacity are oral, keyed, and written, commonly referred to as "taking a test." Educators still do not know, however, the extent to which performance matches capacity.

In the 1980s and '90s, scholarly work in psychological science in the United States started to return to the interests that some have associated with Wundt's early laboratory experiments. In this regard, most recent interest has paired investigations of *mood, imagination,* and *emotions* with memory (Byrnes 2001; Gary and Polaschek 2000; Halgren and Marinkovic 1995; Eysenck and Byrne 1994; Oakhill 1984).

CHILDREN ATTENDING

Vygotsky viewed attention as an essential step in childhood learning, and theorized it in two dimensions. In childhood perceptions, Vygotsky suggested that a *natural attention* was the first phenomenon to occur primarily for here-and-now needs for childhood experiences. Later came a higher order of attention to enable the integration of symbolic meanings that were closely linked to the initial natural attention. In the developmental process, children advance from natural attention to the use of a combined *natural/higher order attention* process (Vygotsky 1930).

This transition, according to Vygotsky, provided an internal understanding of language, language being closely interrelated with thought. The childhood acquisition of language, as explained by Piaget, emerges along with object relations and concrete operations. Here, children are enabled to move beyond egocentrism to a view of objects, events, and categories existing in their own present, past, and future.

Vygotsky was critical of Piaget's developmental approach to childhood attending through their acquisition of knowledge of "concrete operations" and the physical world. Vygotsky described a *zone of proximal development* as the primary source of childhood acquisition of language. He emphasized experiences provided by older individuals and adults in the interacting environment as the primary source of early childhood development.

The zone of proximal development identifies the potential that adult interaction with the child can provide, compared to children acting with each other or alone. The obvious answer is that, under certain circumstances, children can benefit more from interactions with socially experienced adults than with children who have no more experience than themselves.

In an environment where caregivers participate in a language-interactive environment, Vygotsky explains that an environment or "zone" of intentional supportive communication by caregivers encourages growth. More often than not, the give and take of these experiences requires adult responses that are commensurate with the child's level of understanding (maturation). According to Vygotsky, these adult/child experiences encouraged attending because children are participants in their own learning. New knowledge gained from their interactions with caregivers can now be paired with information emerging from regular experiences, the results being advancement in knowledge. Vygotsky explained that children's interactive play often provides these experiences.

Developmental Issues and Attention

Among children in the pre-K to first grade, developmental components of *visual* and *auditory* acuity might not be fully functioning at the time of preschool. VanOeffelen and Vos (1987) have reported that children age four and younger can be confused when they attend to moving objects. Auditory acuity is more fully developed at this age than is visual acuity. However, the ability to isolate certain sounds from others can compete with the teacher's voice and confuse preschoolers when they are trying to attend to a single tone among mixed sounds in an active "open classroom."

A significant number of preschool children, for developmental reasons, might have trouble tracking and coordinating the focus of each eye in a binocular fashion. This inability can account for initial difficulties in reading because of problems in attending to lines of print on a page (Harley and Lawrence 1984).

Occasionally, the teacher, in an attempt to demonstrate the need for paying attention, will ask a complex question that should have required the student's attention of a student who appears to be attending elsewhere. Frequently, the teacher is surprised that, despite the appearance of being completely preoccupied, the child responds with a correct and thoughtful answer. This episode occurs, more often than not, between teachers and students who have been classified as ADHD (attention deficit hyperactive disorder) or autistic. ADHD is discussed in a separate section at the end of this chapter.

Children give the appearance of benefiting from planned experiences (lessons) when their observed behaviors mimic what we have come to believe is attending. Misleading assumptions can accrue in the differences between what the child demonstrates as a response to a planned experience and what is actually occurring at the sensory level of the attention process. Learners who display assumed behaviors of attending and are not necessarily attending in this event, at the same time might be deriving personalized meanings—not necessarily the intended meanings promoted in the lesson. In other words, an appearance of quietly listening, accompanied with a stare, does not necessarily mean that attention is being granted to the intended act. Studies and teacher observations have reported that atypical learners are actually attending while they might be engaged in behaviors that are commonly thought to imply nonattending (Landau, Lorch, and Milich 1992).

Early Child Development and Attention

Ruff and Rothbart, in *Attention in Early Development,* have conceptualized the development of attention during childhood around two overlapping domains. On the one hand, they divided attention into three conceptual categories: selectivity, state, and higher-order control. Then they identified two attention systems thought to occur in early development stages: two to three months, nine to twelve months, and eighteen to twenty-four months, and possibly four years (1996).

Understanding attention as a factor of development starting at birth enables professionals who provide classroom experiences to better understand the significance of attention as an essential function of maturation.

Among other things, Ruff and Rothbart highlighted *selectivity* and aspects of the experience to which an individual decides to attend (select). After selectivity, the final stage is *higher-level control.* For this work, we consider the control area of attention as the learner's response to what has been attended and how their reaction to an experience might be influenced by motivation and values.

For the most part, an empirical assessment of attention is not particularly effective when measures quantify assumed behaviors thought to be indicators of attention. We now know that a great deal can be lost when investigations are pursued through approaches based on behaviorism. Such approaches usually seek to quantify observable human responses but ignore affective mental processing.

For example, studies of infants often quantify eye movement to assess individual attention. Whereas the consistent position of the eyes can reveal the direction of the visual track, this provides little information about the underlying purpose of the attention or the nature of information being processed (Fernald 1989).

Let us say that an infant is seated in a testing environment and a picture of the infant's mother is placed in view while all else is shielded from sight. As the infant's attention is analyzed, what are the motivations for or intent of the infant's attention? Does the infant attend to the image because of familiarity with the object (caregiver)? Does this imply that the infant would focus on the picture if it represented a likeness of anyone (human face, pet, etc.)? Is attention given to the picture because of shading contrasts representing new or novel visual experiences for the infant? These and other variables raise uncertainties.

Teachers want their potential learners to place their attention under the influence of their planned experiences (instruction, group work, homework, etc.). After attention has been placed in the service of the classroom experience by the perceiver, access to memory becomes available through the learner's sensory mechanisms. Attention is one of several major variables that can advance or inhibit the learner's willingness, or apparent capacity, to acquire new information and expand what is already known and thereby improve the quality and quantity of their knowledge. Two major views concern the effectiveness of attention. One view is that the perceiver controls attention through valuing and screening; the other is that the perceiver is a passive participant in what is ultimately passed on to the memory system.

HUMAN PROCESSING OF INFORMATION AND EXPERIENCE

Neural processes and the brain are internally located, with no access to the unfolding experiences in the "outside world." Access to "being-in-the-world" experience is provided by the senses.

When teachers are introducing a lesson, they often start with an *attention getter* to encourage learners to attend to the planned experience. When learners decide to attend to an experience, their sensory systems (sight, auditory, olfactory, touch, and taste) are engaged. The development of attention in childhood parallels the development of perception. Attention is directed at something in particular, and this attention employs perception almost immediately.

It is attention that activates the human *perceptual sensory* system. In the phases that follow, human sensory systems submit stimuli selected from an experience to short-term memory for selectivity and processing, then on to the final stage (long-term memory), thus increasing knowledge (Atkinson and Shiffrin 1968).

The brain and neural networks are within the body systems in darkness and must rely on sensory inputs from the organism's external experiences. To what one decides to attend is primarily a choice of the perceiver. Perceptual organs can transmit information from the world of experiences by taste, touch, smell, auditory, and visual sensations. This aspect of information processing is described in chapter 4.

Experiences that capture one's attention also heighten perception to maximize what might be gained from experiences at hand. Without a decision by the student (perceiver) to attend to an experience (in this case, a lesson), the information being transmitted is less likely processed toward long-term memory.

For example, according to their teacher, Mark and Michael are equally bright fourth graders. They are friends who play together after school and frequently do homework together. They seem to grant equal amounts of attention to planned classroom experiences, and often each will know the answer when questions are asked. When standardized tests are given to measure what they have "learned" from classroom experiences, their teacher is disappointed that there is a substantial difference between their scores. Many factors can account for this, including (1) their personal valuing of test performance, (2) differences between their attention and perception of the shared experience, (3) differences in overall motivation, and (4) how each felt on the day of the test.

Among the various classroom teaching models in education, there seems to be common agreement. Differences seem to occur in the interpretations of what constitutes learning, and getting and holding the learner's attention. Learning has occurred when information is stored in, and can be retrieved from, long-term memory.

The processing of information is more complex than the scenario of Mark and Michael. Gender can be a factor in attention and perception, as well as experiences during maturation, like conversations between children and their parents around the dinner table. A child can be concerned that she should not appear too smart because playmates who are not performing well might not like her. It is also true that some children go to homes where being alone is common and they might not know whether or not their parents value teachers or school performance.

Some psychological studies have proposed that individuals have mental capacities for processing information beyond what are now identified as sensory capabilities. These views are commonly found in humanistic psychology and in studies associated with branches of existentialism and phenomenology. By no means do these concepts constitute the whole of humanistic or existential psychology, and this expanded view usually rests on subjective or anecdotal evidence.

For example, in studies of some expanded views, there are reports by individuals who contemplate communicating with a colleague, and shortly thereafter, the individual contemplating the original act receives communication from the intended target. Conclusions are drawn that there is a manner of communication that occurs between individuals or objects that does not require objective experiences or neural sensory pathways. Although work being done in this area might be important to educators and psychologists, integrating such reports into this work is not within the scope of this book.

Undivided attention to tasks and objects is not necessary for all classroom experiences, even for some that are considered complex. In fact, to function well, young children must be selective among the tremendous number of experiences and variations in their lives. Variations can harbor complex ideas and events with meanings that are made clear only after certain levels of maturation are reached (Ruff and Rothbart 1996).

A fifth grader, when in first grade, for example, might have had difficulties in learning to hold a pencil properly to write legibly. Now, writing comes easily for the fifth grader with little or no attention given to the skill. The writer can ignore the mechanics of using the pencil while attending to the content of writing with greater intentionality.

The intentional focus of attention on selected experiences can introduce variables influenced by values and motivation (Dixon and Hertzog 1988). In some cases, these two factors can be supportive of one another. For example, when a class of fifth graders is visiting an art exhibit in their hometown museum, values and motivation can provide a complex interplay for individual children, their teacher, and friendship subgroups in the class.

Analyzing such an experience can provide a wealth of interpretations from a Gestalt and an existential perspective. Let's say that a small subgroup in the class pals around together because their parents are at work when school is dismissed. Further, this same subgroup is advised by their parents to go into the museum after school and wait to be picked up by either parent.

By the time of the class trip to the museum, this small group of after school friends is already well known to the people who run the museum. The museum staff looks with some disfavor upon these daily visitors who occasionally run and romp around the premises. There will be greater familiarity, some trepidation, and some anxiety among individual members of this subgroup that is not present in the current museum experience of other children.

The intentional focus of attention on objects and tasks can introduce a similar (but occasionally different) set of variables when compared to events and problems. The classroom teacher presenting a lesson can be considered an event. Here, if the teacher is discussing family traveling experiences and the variety of activities in which children might participate, this event will capture the attention of children in different ways. The objective of this lesson (experience) might be "language arts." The children are encouraged to suggest a variety of activities that are possible while traveling with one's family (reading a fun book, doing puzzles, telling riddles and jokes, etc.). Class discussion could be followed by a writing assignment and a review of student work. At the end of the day, homework can be assigned that calls for parent/child interaction in the home with a family member.

Different values are brought to this experience by children whose families do not have a car and seldom leave their neighborhoods than by children whose families have a large-size van and have purchased a group pass to a year-round amusement park several hundred miles from their neighborhood.

In this classroom experience, attention will be influenced in different ways by values and motivation. This does not necessarily mean that children in vacation-at-home families will not be motivated to attend to this experience. It means that children will not bring the same values and motivations to the shared experience.

For some children in vacation-at-home families, fantasy might be a strong motivating factor for attending to this experience. Make believe might be a major means of coping with a life confined to their neighborhood, while others in the same set of family circumstances might value the experience less and have little motivation to attend to this particular experience.

When an object or act is valued, its value can be judged as interesting, fascinating, or threatening. Positive valuing can call forth increased vigilance, and therefore increased attention. The positive valuing of an object or event can influence (motivate) a child to attend to that experience. It is also likely that the negative valuing of an object or event can reduce attention (avoidance).

The essential message here is that children, for a variety of reasons, might not attend to an experience when the perceived message has little or no value to them.

Early studies of perception and attention reported that attention to an object might evoke a reaction based on *symbolic value* and could be reacted to in a variety of ways: as a reward, threat to security, pleasure, or punishment, for example (Bruner, Oliver, and Greenfield 1966).

It is also true, however, that the creative use of teaching materials and the excitement that teachers can bring to a classroom experience often overcome obstacles to attention, especially when the educator is aware of the varied possibilities and challenges introduced by concepts of attention.

YOUNG CHILDREN AND
STUDIES OF ATTENTION

There has been some controversy among day-care providers who complain that they must often "re-teach" children how to refer to objects and events correctly after caregiver interaction in the home has encouraged "baby talk." Words like "potty," "tee-tee," and "wee-wee" are common. Studies have reported that babies might naturally prefer attending to speech that has certain features, and that caregivers might respond to these preferences after intuitively recognizing this by observing the infant's attending (Sachs 1977). It has also been reported from studies that most infants prefer attending to baby talk (Werker and McLeod 1989; Cooper and Aslin 1990).

Optimal conditions for the infant's perception of language include the establishment of caregiver/infant eye contact when the infant becomes quiet, faces the speaker, and responds (Prizant and Wetherby 1990).

Several investigators have studied obstacles to attention from the perspective that sometimes obstructions can ultimately improve learning. It has been suggested that distractions can actually lead to improved learning. In this regard, Higgins and Turnure (1984) reported that attention was increased when distracters were introduced, and that act can ultimately lead to improved attending.

In general, distractions as a developmental issue can have a negative influence on "attending" by three-year-old children when they are compared to their four-year-old counterparts. Weissberg, Ruff, and Lawson (1990) have reported that three-year-olds need more reminding to pay attention than do four-year-olds.

In a study that examined attention among infants, five-month-old children were observed while they inspected large geometric patterns. It was reported that "short-lookers" had novelty scores above chance, while "long-lookers" demonstrated less-than-chance scores (Jankowski, Rose, and Feldman 2001).

When attention is studied among young children, important developmental differences should not be overlooked. An experiment that examined visual attention and recognition memory among preterm and full-term infants, varying in ages from five to seven months, reported significant differences in attention between the age groups, and between preterm and full-term infants. The infants also demonstrated consistent *attentional styles*: "short-lookers," "long-lookers," etc. Better recognition was reported for the "short-lookers" and those with higher shift rates (Rose, Feldman, and Jankowski et al. 2001).

In a much earlier study, Sheingold (1973) investigated attentional differences between children of different ages. Various visual stimuli were placed before children of different ages. When the five-year-old children were asked to report on what they observed immediately, they had little difficulty with accuracy. Recollections from their sensory register were almost equal to adults and older children.

After the stimuli were removed, younger children appeared to retain significantly less in their sensory register than adults and children older than five years old. This report seems to indicate that sensory register capacity among the young has a faster decay period when compared to the sensory registers of older children and adults.

Attention creates an original source of knowledge gained from experience. After attending to an experience, perception is the next step, and then a brief storage in the sensory register (Atkinson and Shiffrin 1968). These three stages occur almost simultaneously, to the extent that they can be considered, functionally, a single stage.

The initial "registration" in the sensory store area precedes the entry of information into the second component—short-term memory. In short-term memory, information is assumed to remain for a longer period of time than in the sensory register, but it is still expected to decay completely over time (Estes and Taylor 1966; Sperling 1967).

Sheingold (1973) reported a decline in performance during the sensory register period among children younger than five years, explaining that this finding might have more to do with maturation than with the transfer of information from the sensory register to short-term memory and then to long-term memory.

The storage and retrieval of knowledge follows a complex pattern. Among school-age children, for example, skilled responses to the steps and stages in mathematics comprehension call for a pathway that requires competencies at each interval. Some developmental competencies are influenced by maturation and in part are tied to the learner's "readiness" to understand an experience or selective parts of an experience.

First, the learner's attention is usually drawn to single numbers and later to number combinations. The processing of these otherwise "nonsense symbols" requires prior knowledge of their meanings as symbols. Each number (symbol) has a word to designate its identity with a "name" that is commonly known. In addition to this "name," it also has numerical value not identified by size or color. It is this numerical value that might be the most important feature of the experience now being created for the learner through the teacher's lesson. For this conversation to be meaningful for the perceiver (learner), there must be a shared understanding of the "name" and value of the number being presented.

For the learner, a seemingly simple mathematical presentation requires the retrieval of previous knowledge concerning recognition, identity, and value of the numbers to which the learner might attend. Here, developmentalists suggest that age (maturation) is a factor to consider because the symbolic meaning of a number is a social concept as well as a numerical one. For children in the preoperational stage, each number is a single entity, in that the number five is a single symbol, as is the number three. The fact that five is considered "more" than three is seldom fully understood by three- to four-year-olds because each number is a single item. Even when numbers are spread out as single objects, the "spread" will determine the meaning of "more" rather than the symbolic meaning of the number. This example demonstrates the close relationship between attending and perception.

Sometimes in the presence of family members, parents of very young children encourage them to display a number of fingers by asking, "How old are you?" Children can usually complete this act rather accurately. In their conceptual understanding of number, each finger is separate with its own "name" (one, two, three, etc.). As a group, their fingers have no cumulative value. Until children reach the age of four or five, however, they do not fully understand the cumulative concept of numbers. This is explained in Piaget's concept of object permanence (Piaget 1954) and highlights the idea that it is important for teachers to be knowledgeable about the personal range of reality that young learners bring to an experience.

Parault and Schwanenflugel (2000) studied developmental aspects of children's conceptual understanding of attention. The study reported three conceptual stages that appear to increase with age: (1) surface features of scenarios used in similarity judgments receive less emphasis, (2) more attentional subtypes are identified, and (3) the role of effort in attention receives more emphasis.

Surface features and the appearance of objects have also been of interest to other investigators. In this regard, a three-part study reported that children attended exclusively to the appearances of objects while learning nouns in the context of moving objects. While learning verbs, however, children attended equally to appearances and motions. When objects were familiar (as opposed to novel objects), children attended more to objects in motion than to object appearance. The primary purpose of this study was to examine the extent to which the attention of preschool children attended to objects or actions while learning a novel verb (Kersten and Smith 2002).

The extent to which reading disabilities might be associated with oculomotor readiness was observed by Solan and others (2001). They studied the relationship between eye movement and concentration of students while they were reading. Eye-movement therapy and reading-comprehension techniques were administered to a group of children over a period of twelve weeks. At the end of that period, a total reading growth of 2.6 years was reported.

In another examination of attention among young learners, the time of day for optimal advantage for attention from fifth graders and tenth graders was studied. It was reported that attentional levels were particularly high among fifth graders in the afternoon. It was also reported that high levels of attention for tenth graders occurred in the afternoon (Klein 2001).

In classroom activities designed for the gifted, students are often occupied with more than a single task. Irwin-Chase and Burns, in studies involving two experiments, investigated age differences when attention to dual tasks was expected (2000). The study reported that when single-task performance was controlled, there were no differences found when fifth graders were compared to second graders in the differentiation and allocation of attention to tasks. When priorities for the tasks were set, only fifth graders could differentiate in task allocation of attention.

Vygotsky viewed attention as an essential step in child development and theorized it in two dimensions. In childhood perceptions, Vygotsky suggested that a natural attention was the first phenomenon to occur primarily for the here-and-now needs in childhood experiences. Later came a higher order of attention to enable the integration of symbolic meanings that were closely linked to the initial natural attention. In the developmental process, children advance from natural attention to the use of a combined natural/higher-order attention process (Vygotsky 1930).

This developmental transition, according to Vygotsky, followed the child's internalization of language learning. This stage is closely related to the childhood acquisition of language and Piaget's concrete operations stage. Here, children are enabled to move beyond egocentrism in their conceptualization of self, to the perception of objects and categories existing in a present, future, and a past (Piaget 1954).

LEARNERS WHO CANNOT
OR WILL NOT ATTEND

Attention deficit hyperactivity disorder (ADHD) has become the common label for children who cannot, or will not, attend. Identifying this group goes far beyond a mere label. Early studies have identified this group as impulsive, hyperactive, minimally brain damaged, and with an attention deficit disorder (ADD).

This problem of attention diversion has been a major focus of special education for some time now, and the number of children labeled as ADD/ADHD is growing.

Many educators of learners with special needs have concluded that there are learners who simply cannot attend. This group of learners is described by teachers as unable to pay attention to assigned classroom tasks for reasonable periods of time. Today, many of these children are diagnosed as learners with attention deficit disorder (ADD).

Among children diagnosed with ADHD, attending is also a major concern of parents and teachers. It is common to describe this group as hyperactive and inattentive. It has been reported that distractions during learning activities might provide an alternative schooling environment for hyperactive children.

Lack of attention, however, is not the only behavior to which classroom teachers and parents object. There are diagnostic variations in the national approach by professionals in characterizing a group of disorders associated with inattention and hyperactivity.

However, various characteristics are commonly accepted as ADHD. The most common characteristics are:

- Inability or unwillingness to attend to schoolwork long enough to complete a task.

- Difficulty in sorting and/or organizing tasks to reach satisfactory completion.
- Frequently in motion and easily distracted and/or diverted from assigned tasks.
- Appearing to comprehend instructions, but infrequently following through.
- Frequently in motion even while seated; twisting, turning, and dropping objects.
- Impulsive approach to problem solving; willing to sacrifice accuracy for speed.

Researchers investigated the effects that distractions might have upon the attention of a group of hyperactive boys. A group of six- to twelve-year-old boys was invited into a controlled setting where a TV was showing an educational program. When toys were introduced to this group, the attention of the hyperactive boys appeared to turn away from the educational program and toward the toys. While preoccupied with toys, the hyperactive boys appeared to attend indirectly to the TV program half as much as the nonhyperactive boys.

Despite the appearance that the hyperactive boys were not attending to the educational program, the recall of information from the educational program was similar for both groups (Landau, Lorch, and Milich 1992).

In this study, using the extent to which children are otherwise occupied as an indicator of attention was misleading. The half-time attention of the hyperactive group might also be an indicator of a useful alternative approach to creating effective learning environments for children diagnosed with attention deficits.

ATTENTION AND HYPERACTIVE DISORDERS, A HISTORY

As early as 1929, Harthshorne, May, and Miller discussed the childhood problem of self-control. In some schools during this time, some parents were being asked to keep children at home who could not attend to the lessons. At the same time, other investigators paired inattention with "inhibition," "anxiety," and "motor-deliberation."

In 1938, H. A. Murray, in his book *Explorations in Personality*, labeled inattention and hyperactive characteristics as "impulsive deliberation." By 1959, using observed behavior as primary criteria, Sutton-Smith and Rosenberg developed a scale to identify children who met certain criteria as *impulsive childhood dysfunction*. Labeled *attention deficit hyperactivity disorder* today, the Sutton-Smith Rosenberg scale employed a single-step procedure that identified, within a specified group, only those who could be labeled *impulsive*; it was then assumed that the remaining children in that group were *not impulsive*.

For various complex reasons, from the early 1950s, impulsivity, hyperactivity, and attention deficit disorder were consistently mentioned in various ways in clinical descriptions. In 1996, children who had been previously labeled *minimal brain hyperactive* (MBH) and *attentional deficit hyperactive* (ADH) were being diagnosed as having an *attention deficit disorder with hyperactivity* (ADDH).

Characteristics of this latter group were remarkably similar to children defined earlier as MBD and ADD, sometimes including characteristics such as "inattentiveness," "failure to complete tasks," "unable (or unwilling) to concentrate," "impulsiveness," and "frequent shifting of interests and attention."

By the 1990s, ADDH settled into professional and public literature as attention deficit hyperactivity disorder (ADHD) while published symptoms remained the same.

There seemed to be concerted efforts by school authorities, frustrated parents, drug companies, and physicians to match diagnosis and treatment to accommodate childhood behaviors that appeared troublesome for some teachers and parents. The list of these "behaviors" labeled as "symptoms" tended to grow annually.

In 1994, scholars were still engaged in trying to disentangle the attention deficit paradigm from a general dysfunctional context. That year, an important study was published that asked a significant question in its title, *When Is "Impulsiveness" Not Impulsive? The Case of Hyperactive Children's Cognitive Style*. In introducing this study, Sonuga-Barke, Houlberg, and Hall informed us that:

Philosophers of science have become increasingly aware of the way in which normative assumptions embodied in scientific terminology influence research strategy. This is particularly clear in the human sciences where terms are often borrowed from everyday speech. For instance, the term *impulsive*, when understood as a symptom of childhood psychopathology, has both a descriptive and an explanatory significance. It couples a description of a response in favor of immediacy and certain assumptions about both the dysfunctional character and the constitutional origins of that response. In short, the assumption is that children "don't wait not because they don't want to wait but because they can't wait." In this way, hyperactive children's apparently maladaptive and unconditional preference for response or reward immediacy has been assumed by psychopathologists to reflect a deficit in regulative functioning or inhibitory processes thought by many to lie at the heart of their problem. (1994, 1247–48)

By 1996, amid a serious debate among professionals regarding prescribing excessive drugs for children, popular media reported that more than three million children in the United States, mostly boys, had been diagnosed as having ADHD. Over 60 percent of children diagnosed as ADHD were prescribed drugs (primarily Ritalin) and the remainder were treated through behavior modification and family therapy. Several studies have reported that hyperactivity in young children often disappears with adolescent maturation. It has also been suggested that academic and emotional problems can persist and these children remain on medication for reasons more related to inattention and impulsivity than hyperactivity (Laufer 1962; Menkes, Rowe, and Menkes 1967; Cohen, Weiss, and Minde 1972).

For those children and parents seeking family therapy for attention deficit and hyperactivity, the reports are mixed. Today, childhood psychological problems are sometimes dealt with in a school setting with a team that includes a counselor, psychologist, social worker, and when possible, the teacher.

Few schools have psychologists and social workers on staff. When they are on staff, their assignment usually includes several schools. Under such circumstances, their role is primarily to assist other school personnel to deal with problems of children by conducting workshops in schools, making referrals of the more serious problems to outside agencies, and administering individual tests to support referrals. School counselors are usually assigned tasks that do not include working on problems with individual children.

Schools now have the legal right to refuse school admission to children who have been diagnosed with ADHD unless they submit to drug treatment. Some schools will accept family therapy without drug treatment while others will not.

For many families, talk therapy (family therapy), sometimes offered on a referral basis through the school, has provided a useful service. It has been reported that ADHD children tend to respond to family therapy as they mature, and are able to operate on their own when they reach their mid-teens.

Often providing a long-term expensive process, family therapy has had a long and uneven history. Early in the 1900s, childhood behavior problems were viewed as one aspect of family dysfunction. From the influence of Sigmund Freud and his daughter, Anna Freud, psychoanalysts in the United States sought understandings of child development primarily from their adult clients' descriptions of their own childhood.

Family therapy is no longer limited to the relationships between family members, nor is it limited to school and home. Haley and associates have expanded the original family therapy concepts considerably.

There is an increasing awareness that psychiatric problems are social problems that involve the total ecological system. There is concern with, and an attempt to change, what happens within the family and also the interlocking systems of the family and the social institutions in which the family is embedded. The fragmentation of the individual into parts is being abandoned, and there is growing consensus calling for a new ecological framework defining problems in new ways and for new ways in therapy (Haley 1972, 270).

During these early years, treatment modalities continued over such extended periods of time that it was not unusual for families to be in therapy long after they were no longer in contact with the social worker or teacher who referred them in the first place. Teachers and school authorities were growing impatient with this psychosocial model that relied upon "talk therapy" and were poised for fewer time-consuming methods to deal with troublesome pupils.

During the 1940s, mental institutions for adults were also being criticized from within the professions by advocacy groups and from the general public because of the use of restraining devices and isolation cells to maintain seriously disruptive mental patients. By the 1950s, remarkable results were emerging from the use of drugs that dramatically reduced the acting-out behavior of adult psychotic patients. The success of antipsychotic drugs for the treatment of adult mental disorders was accompanied by studies investigating how these treatments affected the brain and central nervous system.

Investigations along these lines were enhanced through the use of the electroencephalogram (EEG) to study institutionalized youth and adults. This activity attracted the attention of the psychologists and social workers who worked with troubled families and youth having problems in school. Gradually, talk therapy as a treatment for the problems of troubled youth would be partially abandoned in favor of a drug treatment that had proved successful with troublesome institutionalized patients. For institutionalized adults, the new drug treatment was a part of a larger program to release them into their community with appropriate medication. Many social agencies believe that this policy led to the increase in homelessness in the 1980s.

These trends created a professional climate that gradually employed the medical model in the treatment of child development problems and a gradual reduction in the use of the Freudian "dysfunctional family" approach, which previously required extensive social work and psychoanalysis.

Along with the aforementioned developments, and throughout the 1960s, greater interest grew in the relationship between brain function and abnormal behavior in children. EEG data were used to develop profiles of brain-damaged children from examinations of those who had been institutionalized for various reasons. From these investigations, and as early as 1955, Ounsted described epileptic children in the same clinical contexts with children who demonstrated *pervasive short attention span, aggressive outbursts,* and children who were labeled *distractible.*

Following the great success that institutions were having with the use of tranquilizing drugs to calm patients who previously had to be isolated or physically restrained, the medical community, universities, governmental health agencies, and drug companies sponsored workshops, institutes, and conferences aimed at expanding the application for psychoactive behavior-altering drugs. Members of the medical community usually associated with child development, such as psychiatrists and pediatricians, gradually introduced the term *minimal brain dysfunction* to bring into their sphere the diagnosis and treatment of the school's most chronic behavioral problems as neurological and not psychosocial.

Throughout the 1960s, psychiatric literature identifying minimal brain dysfunction as a neurological problem listed various behaviors as common symptoms for which educators and practitioners should be on the alert. S. D. Clements not only authored a health service bulletin for the U.S. Department of Health Education and Welfare titled "Minimal Brain Dysfunction in Children" but authored and coauthored many scientific reports on the subject. Among the common characteristics of MBD that were cited in Clement's work were "impulsivity," "hyperactivity," "short attention span," and "distractibility."

These developments had been aided in 1966 by the creation of a task force by the National Institute of Neurological Diseases and Blindness to develop a diagnostic term for children who demonstrated compulsive inattentive behavior that was generally troublesome for parents and teachers. The task force had created the term *minimal brain dysfunction*. The word *minimal* was important here because, at that time, no significant neurological evidence was found to substantiate such a distinction. Previous terms like *neurological disorder, hyperactivity*, and *brain damage* were now included under minimal brain dysfunction diagnoses.

The practice of employing pathological labels to officially group childhood *impulsivity* among other behaviors diagnosed as *attention deficit, hyperkinetic,* or *hyperactive* created an enormous market for the sale of medications purported to control the undesirable acting-out behavior of children. The American Psychiatric Association had by now created *hyperkinetic syndrome of childhood* as the official descriptor for the research, diagnosis, and treatment of these disorders in children.

Throughout the 1970s, this "official" label was conveniently available to physicians, teachers, and other school personnel who were exasperated with children whose classroom demeanor was inattentive and generally annoying. Parents, some of whom had only a minimal understanding of the subject from popular media, made frequent requests to physicians to prescribe Ritalin for their children so that "they will get better grades in school."

By 1980, it was estimated that over one million schoolchildren, mostly boys, were regularly prescribed drugs to modify their inattentive behavior in school. The scientific community discovered that the body's normal flow of dopamine to the frontal lobe of the brain served to regulate impulsivity and attention. Without any direct evidence that children demonstrating impulsive or inattentive behavior had an organic problem related to frontal lobe dysfunction, the modified behavior induced by various drugs that increased the flow of dopamine to the brain was sufficient justification for their use. The most popularly prescribed drugs were Dexedrine (dextroamphetamine), Ritalin (methylphenidate), and Cylert (permoline).

Companies that profited from the sale of these drugs mailed an avalanche of literature to physicians; sponsored research projects, professional seminars, and workshops; and sent professionals to address parent–teacher meetings to promote the use of their products.

A persistent lack of clinical evidence existed to confirm a hard link between specific central nervous system dysfunction and the listed behaviors that were attached to the hyperkinetic syndrome, under which tremendous amounts of psychoactive drugs were being dispensed to children. Annually, the number of children between the ages of five and seventeen who were diagnosed as hyperkinetic or hyperactive began to experience a rapid growth after 1970. A relatively small number of pediatricians, psychologists, psychiatrists, parents, and educators were becoming alarmed at the high rate of schoolchildren who were being given behavior-controlling medication, and they started to question the practice of labeling inattentive impulsive behavior as a brain disorder.

In 1975, Peter Schrag and Diane Divoky wrote an important book, *The Myth of the Hyperactive Child: And Other Means of Child Control,* that captured the attention of professionals and parents. The timing of their publication witnessed troubling increases in medical diagnoses of hyperactivity, inattentiveness, and minimal brain dysfunction.

> In less than a decade, the ailment spread from virtual obscurity to something well beyond epidemic proportions. It has no single name, no universally accepted symptoms, and no discernible anatomical or biochemical

characteristics which can be diagnosed in a clinic or laboratory, yet it is said to affect as many as 40 percent of all American children, to reflect an organic or chemical dysfunction of the brain or the nervous system and to be the cause of most, if not all, pediatric problems in learning and behavior. Its most common name . . . is "learning disabilities" (LD) . . . sometimes synonymous with "minimal brain dysfunction" (MBD), "hyperkinesis," "impulse disorder," and a substantial number of other conditions and "syndromes." (1975, 30)

The Schrag and Divoky publication created a great deal of interest among parents with school-age children and the general public. As is often the case, concerns of the general public can stir interest in the professional community and stimulate research activity where little or none previously existed. The practice of medicating schoolchildren to reduce their fidgety inattention is now more than a quarter of a century old.

In this regard, some of the more interesting research literature appeared after the work of Schrag and Divoky. Among those studies that questioned the practice of utilizing broad and inclusive childhood behaviors as descriptions for highly active children, Schachar, Rutter, and Smith pointed out that:

The very existence of "hyperactivity" as a behavior which is independent of the observer value system has been called into question. It has been argued that the diagnosis is no more than an artificially created "medical" label applied to children whose behavior is annoying to adults because it does not comply with the demands of the home or school environment. This definition of the "hyperkinetic syndrome" has also been challenged empirically. Studies have failed to demonstrate the interrelatedness of the behaviors usually attributed to the syndrome. . . . The concept of the syndrome has also been challenged on clinical grounds. . . . In Great Britain and Europe, clinicians have tended to reserve the diagnosis of "hyperkinetic syndrome" for the very few children who show severe overactivity and inattentiveness in nearly all situations. (1981, 376)

Without much discussion to the contrary among the public, it is assumed to be a natural impulse that children should be attending when adults are presenting. This inclination to harshly criticize those children who might make choices for their own attention that are unlike those made by adults for them seems common among parents, teachers, and school authorities. By the 1960s, such criticisms concerning children's attentiveness in school reached a crisis proportion.

Among the most troublesome behaviors that tended to unnerve parents and teachers was a child's lack of attention to assigned classroom tasks. It was only a matter of time before the professional community would recognize this and eventually incorporate it among its growing litany of drug-treatable symptoms.

In the 1960s, prescriptions for hyperactivity as a brain disorder frequently employed the term *distractibility.* By 1980, minimal brain dysfunction was expanded to include attention deficit disorder, marking a point when the therapeutic community expanded the pool of children well beyond the earlier American Psychiatric Association's diagnostic label of the hyperkinetic childhood syndrome.

The inability or refusal by a pupil to sustain attention in the classroom was thought to be a neurological deficit, referred to as *a lack of sustained attention* among educators, psychiatrists, and psychologists, and gradually became the centerpiece of treatable hyperactive behavior in children. In the 1990s, the research community focused considerably on issues related to attention deficit disorders.

> A sustained attention deficit is thought by many to be the cardinal component of hyperactivity. On tests of vigilance, lasting anything from 5 to 30 min., hyperactive children tend to have poorer concentration and so make many more mistakes in absolute terms than control children. However, poor performance on vigilance tasks does not necessarily imply a sustained attention deficit. The greater number of errors made by hyperactive children may be due to a whole host of unrelated motivational and cognitive variables. In order to isolate such a deficit one must show that hyperactive children's attention decays more quickly over time than that of non-hyperactive controls. (Sonuga-Barke and Taylor 1992, 1091)

Since the 1950s, impulsivity and inattention has been entangled with labels attributed to diagnosed behaviors such as *distractible, hyperkinetic, attention deficit,* and *hyperactive.* The etiology of trends that created a dysfunction context for the use of brain-altering drugs like Ritalin appears to emerge for helping children, while in reality, they are employed to reduce frustration among teachers and parents. Some physicians will not prescribe drugs like Ritalin and Cylert; parents and school authorities, however, quickly learn the names and locations of physicians who will.

It still remains difficult for educators to view inattention as a desirable trait because of the often high error rate in students' schoolwork. There are studies, however, that attempt to separate learners who approach their schoolwork with intensity and sincerity of early resolution, and those who lack the control to perform in any other way (Meichenbaum and Goodman 1969; Heider 1971).

It is also likely, if given the choice, that teachers prefer students who are reflective, thoughtful, and patient. Such characteristics seem to embody all that is good about scholarship in particular and academia in general. Because this is probably true, Mischel (1974) and Meredith (1978) have focused upon inattentive and impulsive information-processing styles by orienting individuals to become more reflective and deliberate in their attention to schoolwork. This ultimately is more successful in resolving the requirements placed upon them by their school (Egeland 1974). Scholars who have reported a lack of directed attention can be misdiagnosed as a clinical form of hyperactivity (Cohen, Weiss, and Minde 1972).

In the current literature, the discussion concerning attention deficit has centered around two major foci: one raises the question concerning attention *deficit*, the other is on the problem of individual *control* of attention (Schachar and Gordon 1991). Several studies have taken positions against the deficit model. A major feature of this point of view emerges from what we have learned about attention since it was highlighted in the 1960s. We now know that there are different types of attention, and even the more common types, such as sustained attention, divided attention, and attentional capacity, have been delineated in studies.

In general, the present-day conceptualization of ADHD with attention perceived as a unitary entity is being challenged (Schachar & Logan 1991; Barkley 1990). Norman and Shallice (1986) introduced a concept of *supervisory attentional control* labeled *supervisory attentional system*

(SAT). It provides a more elaborate role for the higher-level control of working memory. ADHD continues to be a very active area for scholarly investigations. Important ideas concerning attention deficits are continually emerging, including recent reports that as people mature, ADHD tends to disappear (Barkley 1981; Shaffer 1994).

THREE

Perception

Perception is manifestly an activity which seeks to satisfy standards which it sets to itself. The muscles of the eye adjust the thickness of its lens, so as to produce the sharpest possible retinal image of the subject on which the viewer's attention is directed, and the eye presents to him as correct the picture of the object seen in this way. This effort anticipates the manner in which we strive for understanding and satisfy our desire for it, by seeking to frame conceptions of the greatest possible clarity.

—Michael Polanyi

For educators, perception is a process through which the human organism selects sensory information derived from experiences. Until the 1960s, perception was not considered a significant part of the cognitive process of thinking and memory. It was thought that perception had an important functional role, and could occur in the absence of intellectual or thinking processes (Gibson 1963). This thinking was influenced by the then-popular *Gestalt* psychologists in their focus on structure and function of perception. This is covered in greater detail later in this chapter.

Associations between children's perception during classroom learning and related academic matters also attracted the attention of educators in the 1960s (Gibson 1965; Kephart 1960). It was Jean Piaget, however, who integrated interpretations of human perceptual sensations into theories of child development (Piaget and Inhelder 1948; Elkind, Koegler, and Go 1962). Piaget was also highly critical of the functional approach to perception that, at least in part, defined Gestaltism (Piaget and Inhelder 1969).

Despite the fact that educators were focusing on children's perception of subject matter experiences, concerns were still directed to the functional visual mechanisms rather than thoughtful selectivity of information from experiences (Gibson 1966; Pick 1965).

For psychologists, perception, in part, selects information from experiences, and the cognitive process organizes this information into meaning. In psychology, when differences are found in the perceptual interpretations of an experience by individuals sharing the same experience, such differences are often attributed to personality variability.

In *phenomenology*, individual perceptual interpretation of an experience, despite its subjectivity, is accepted as an important indicator of a valid human condition. Phenomenology as psychological philosophy is covered later in this chapter.

In the functional sense, perception is the intake of information from all of the sensory inputs—auditory, visual, tactile, taste, and olfactory.

As with attention and memory, experiences take on meaning when the here-and-now input is interpreted through the lens of information that has been gathered over time from previous experiences, and stored in long-term memory.

Experiences occur as individuals go on with their daily lives encountering a variety of different environments. Teachers plan environments and experiences for children. Children are also interested in experiences derived from other environments, such as family or traveling to and from school, as well as being active in the neighborhood and places of significance where experiences are free flowing and not predetermined.

The classroom creates a planned environment where children are expected to gain knowledge from planned experiences. Perception selects information from ongoing experiences of all sorts, as the organism makes meaning by pairing new raw information with knowledge gained from previous experiences.

PERCEPTION AND PHILOSOPHY

Perception and individual interpretations of experiences are found in psychological studies of *phenomenology, existentialism,* and *Gestaltism* (a German word for pattern or configuration). The subjective examination of experience and the perception of an experience are fundamental to phenomenology and existentialism. Existential and phenomenological theories would find objectivity in perceptual interpretations of experiences to be invalid, whereas subjective interpretations of an experience by the perceiver would be accepted as valid. Validity in educational research usually refers to the extent to which test scores enable a conclusion with which other professionals agree. In phenomenology, validity, to the extent that it is relevant, is in the *interpretation of the perceiver.*

For example, as a reward for exceptional performance on a test, a group of children is allowed to play a game of its choosing in the school playground. The teacher supervisor of the playground is impressed with how well the game is going. After an hour of play, a loud disturbance erupts. The rewarding teacher is surprised when this group of children, who usually gets along rather well, becomes disruptive during a pleasurable activity. The teacher was anxious to get an explanation of this *phenomenon*. In her pursuit of the "truth," the teacher takes each child away from the group and asks the same question about how the game became so disruptive. Student responses are hardly helpful for an explanation suitable for the teacher because each student tells a somewhat different story. Some differ slightly and others drift far afield. *Phenomenologists* would explain that different stories are derived from perceptions that logically vary because perceivers bring different life experiences to the phenomenon. In that sense, they are all "truthful." The *perceiver* is more important than the *perceived*. *Existentialists* would agree, with the addition that students are responsible for each other's and their own perceptions.

Phenomenology and existentialism, though significantly different, are frequently paired. Existentialism was popularized by Jean-Paul Sartre (1905–1980), but Martin Heidegger (1889–1976), Karl Jaspers (1883–1969), and Søren Kierkegaard (1813–1855) are the philosophers more associated with existentialism by scholars. Common themes among existentialists often rest upon human conditions associated with dread, discomfort, and tragedy. Existential interpretations associated with these themes include unlimited variations of intent, freedom, and individuality. It is the vast variability between the works of existentialists that confuses comparisons and differentiations (Brentano 1973; Freire 1972; Heidegger 1962).

Sartre (a leftist political activist), Kierkegaard (a Christian), and Heidegger's support for Adolf Hitler confuse attempts at groupings and comparisons. There were, however, remnants of common themes that prevailed often enough in their writings and other works to group the aforementioned individuals as existentialists.

Among the phenomenologists, Franz Brentano (1838–1917) and Edmund Husserl (1859–1938) are most frequently mentioned when the two philosophies are discussed independently. Emerging from the work of philosopher Franz Brentano, phenomenology was introduced as a psychical phenomenon explained through *intentionality*. Brentano explained that mental energy is always *intentionally* directed at something (Brentano 1973).

During the 1960s and '70s, as scholars of theory and philosophy observed the demise of behaviorism, education scholars experienced greater acceptance as they integrated subjective foundations of theory and practice into education philosophy and thought (Morris 1966; Greene 1973). Also in the 1970s, education philosophers revived intentionality (Greene 1978; Zaner and Ihde 1973). During the same period, David Denton's *Existentialism and Phenomenology of Education* described a teacher's perception of work through the lenses of phenomenology and existentialism:

> We plunge into contingency, ambiguity, and tensionality. We bodyforth into a sphere of intentionality and nihilation. We step into the surge of reverberations of a particular lived-reality. Into this abyss of madness, of apparent nonsense, we throw concepts and words and terms in an attempt to provide a meaningful structure. We attempt order with schedules and outlines. We try to explain it all. We set forth role descriptions. We operationalize our terms in an effort to quantify that which is going on. Out of these attempts come formulas, or, to use Goodman's term, formats for teaching, methods for researching teaching, and numerous conceptual analyses of the talk about teaching. That person who wishes to be called teacher soon develops a facility for differentiating among arguments for and against competing formulas. According to the formats, teaching is communication, modifying behavior, classroom management, serving as a resource person, guiding youth, influencing society's tomorrow, function-

ing as a change agent, processing information, establishing I–Thou relationships, et cetera, et cetera, et cetera.

With one or more of the formats in hand, our new teacher walks into
the classroom and quickly discovers that coercion is necessary to make
the situation conform to method, that police-action is becoming his actual
function, that chronic fatigue is his reward at the end of the day. One day
early or late in his life, he looks on himself as though he were standing
outside the classroom, looking at himself through a closed window. From
that new and sudden perspective, his own movements seem absurd, his
gestures meaningless, and his prior commitments sheer folly. (Denton
1974, 99–100)

Gestaltism embraces the idea that perceptions can be influenced by
the *field*. The field is defined by the context within the viewer's purview.
When the field is a group of individuals, for example, the group as a
field can have meaning beyond the sole membership (size) of the group.
It is often said by Gestaltists that *the whole is greater than the sum of
its equal parts.*

For example, five children are called by their teacher to work together on a science project. As they start to plan the project and make
assignments, it quickly becomes apparent to the teacher that for reasons
unknown, these students are not working well together. Here, Gestaltists would explain that the element recognized by the teacher *as not
working* is the *additional element* that is seldom perceived. The additional element is *the group itself.*

The teacher tries a different group of the same number by substitut-
ing two different students for two of the original. This time, difficulties
of a different type surface.

According to Gestaltists, even if only one member were eliminated to
make the group four, the interaction might be unexpected. The difference between five and four would mean that an odd-numbered group
would become an even numbered-group.

Or, if a student substitute were added to maintain the group at five,
interactions and decisions would change again; this might work well, or
might not. Any arrangement, according to the Gestaltists, would modify
perceptions of and by the group, in addition to the number of individuals in the group. The group, perceived as a field, would constitute an

additional element that is not ordinarily perceived as a part of the original group of five.

PERCEPTION AND SCHOOLING

Classroom experiences introduced to children through well-planned lessons initiate chains of experiences that are perceived. This chain includes stored knowledge from experiences previously committed to memory, as well as ongoing in-school and out-of-school experiences.

Through a variety of experiences that naturally occur in daily life, children by the ninth or tenth grade are made aware of many of life's possibilities and are able to integrate new plausible ideas into what they already know. They can also create *new meanings* that embody their creativity.

For example, because of a previous experience, children at an early age would not be surprised to witness a firefly flash its light in darkness. Around the age of ten, they can even understand the chemistry that produces what is unfolding during this perceptual experience. A thirteen-year-old would witness with disbelief, however, a Peter Pan character taking to flight, whereas a three-year-old would not doubt the possibility of such flight. Piaget frequently reported that children are able to advance in knowledge because of a shared relationship between biology and perception. He explained that *perceptual maturation* enabled learners to make their own meaning in keeping with previously acquired knowledge about how their world works.

PERCEPTION, SCIENCE, POLITICS, AND PUBLIC POLICY

Experiences under various conditions, and during different phases of life, can act to preset our perceptions of experiences yet to come. When the perceptions of persons in power, like the president of the United States, a Nobel laureate, or a university professor, for example, lead them to assume a political or intellectual position, thousands of others are led to believe what they perceive. When teachers influence their students in a similar manner, it is called the *hidden curriculum* (covered later in this text).

Influences from perceptions established as early as Jeffersonian democracy are still with us today. As Jefferson helped phrase our Constitution supporting inalienable human rights, he meant rights for white male citizens, not all citizens. Only white males could own property, and property ownership was required for individual voting rights. His perceptions helped define a life of servitude for black families enslaved on his farm, and children yet to be born—including his own. Today, citizens of the United States still struggle with Jeffersonian democracy and the pernicious black/white racism that prevails in its wake.

During his professional lifetime, in which he had a knighthood bestowed by the queen of England, Sir Cyril Burt supplied the research community with ample evidence to support the view that people with dark skin inherited inferior brains (Burt 1940, 1958, 1959). This idea, promoted in public and professional literature at least once a decade, is embraced by supporters of Jeffersonian democracy (Kamin 1974).

This also gives encouragement to groups and individuals with credentials in education, psychology, and anthropology who promote the Burt hypothesis. Psychologists who shared Burt's perceptions built careers on reporting Burt's work to partially support their own perceptions (Jensen 1969; Herrnstein 1973; Herrnstein and Murray 1994; Itzkoff 1994).

In the late 1970s, Burt's work was reported to be fraudulent. His studies, bolstered mostly by data never collected or analyzed, were fabricated (Dorfman 1978; Rensberger 1979; Hechinger 1979).

> Dr. Burt's research, unquestioned and highly influential before his death in 1971, has been criticized in psychological circles since 1972, when it was first found to contain a number of virtual impossibilities. . . .
>
> Further investigations by the *Sunday Times* and Leon Kamin, a Princeton University psychologist, suggest many additional instances of questionable scientific thought, including biased language, favorably reviewing his own books, using pseudonyms in his own journal and fabricating data. (Rensberger 1976, 9)

Muted criticisms of Burt's work were put forth in the 1950s, and his response was published in a journal that later was reported to have been under his control (Burt 1957).

There remains a few but substantial number of educators, psychologists, and scientists as far afield as transistor researchers who cling to the perception that intelligence is inherited and that people with dark skins and the poor are born with inferior intelligence when compared to others in society (Itzkoff 1994).

First in 1968 and again in 1971, William Shockley, a member of the National Academy of Sciences, proposed through an academy committee that they support a study to determine the role of heredity in human performance. Dr. Shockley, a professor at Stanford University and a Nobel laureate for assisting in the development of the transistor, had been at the center of the IQ argument, having proposed that blacks, from birth, were genetically inferior to whites.

The academy refused the Shockley proposal, stating that it was impossible to determine whether racial differences in performance on IQ tests are genetic or environmental (Turner 1972).

One counterperception suggests that the parceling out of performance percentages for environment versus percentages for genetics is an inadequate paradigm from which to obtain useful scientific information.

The discussion, if it should take place at all, should be "bottom up" (that is, a focus on the relationships between biology and the environment in creating total growth and development) rather than "top down" (that is, divide the human pool based on ethnicity and color, then compare the intelligence of groups after they are grown).

Burt, acting on deeply embedded perceptions he never thought necessary to validate, promoted an inclination that remains in the minds of many today. Because the Burt story surfaced in the 1970s, very few textbooks in our 2003 university classrooms mention Burt's fraudulent work when describing intelligence.

The decade of the 1990s witnessed another media blitz to promote the same basic idea—that blacks, and the poor in general, inherit inferior brains. Herrnstein and his graduate student Murray published *The Bell Curve* in 1994. Again, questions arose regarding the use of unsubstantiated data in the book and the use of false reports.

A. L. Pons did test 1,001 Zambial copper miners . . . his data were summarized in a tabular form in a paper by D. H. Crawford-Nutt. Lynn took the Pons data from Crawford-Nutt's paper and converted the number of correct responses into a bogus average "IQ" of 75. Lynn chose to ignore the substance of Crawford-Nutt's paper, which reported that 228 black high school students in Soweto scored an average of 45 correct responses . . . higher than the mean of 44 achieved by the same-age white sample. (Kamin 1995, 100)

In responding to the intentions of the nature of content dissemination found in these distorted reports, Kamin wrote:

> Lynn's distortions and misrepresentations of the data constitute a truly venomous racism, combined with scandalous disregard for scientific objectivity. Lynn is widely known among academicians to be an associate editor of the racist journal *Mankind Quarterly* and a major recipient of financial support from the nativists' eugenically oriented Pioneer Fund. It is a shame and a disgrace that two eminent social scientists, fully aware of the sensitivity of the issue they address, take Lynn as their scientific tutor and uncritically accept his surveys of research. (Kamin 1995, 100)

It is proposed among a substantial group of scholars that scientific inquiry should not be inhibited merely because it raises uncomfortable questions and can lead to unintended consequences. Many in this same group who support investigations of black/white differences reject scientific inquiry into possible differences between Italians and Germans, English and French, and Russians and Polish, for example (Hacker 1994).

Andrew Hacker suggests that negative perceptions based on race are not new, and should not be surprising. He reports that white scholars agreed some time ago not to make genetic distinctions between groups of white residents in the United States. Blacks, on the other hand, remain an accessible and desirable target for negative reporting "because it is better for white sensibilities, to focus on presumed black inefficiencies" (Hacker 1994).

Kamin suggests that the persistent perception of inferiority of blacks, poor, and recent immigrants is influenced by questionable science and opportunistic politicians (1974).

DEVELOPMENTAL STAGES AND PERCEPTION

Piaget and other developmentalists reported from their work that children cannot accurately interpret what they perceive (concrete operations) until they are around six years of age. Erikson cites the same age for childhood perception of the relationship between themselves and the rest of the world. This is the developmental stage that Erikson identifies as a period when childhood concerns start to turn outward from family toward social entities like school, peers, and community. Freud defined the ages of six to nine years as a sexually latent period. Others have reported that children in the United States achieve this capacity a year earlier.

During Freud's Oedipal stage (a period of sibling rivalry), conflicts naturally emerge between parents and their children of the same gender. This stage ends around age six, introducing the developing child to the less tumultuous *latent* period. Though influenced by sexual discussions in literature, a more appropriate view of Freud's work would identify his sexual connotations as *gender* related.

Behaviorists like Watson and Skinner would take a different tack. They rely primarily on the control of experiences selected for their likelihood of producing predetermined, socially desirable behaviors.

Piaget, Freud, and Erikson viewed knowledge derived from experiences as information screened through a learner's developmental readiness to process such knowledge (in part or whole). Behaviorists, on the other hand, ignored perceptional variability, and theorized that the careful design and control of perception, as well as the experience, would provide the most effective means for implanting information.

Except for D. O. Hebb (1972), behaviorists expressed little interest in the neural processes in knowledge acquisition. For a period, the role of neurons, dendrites, and axons in the processing of information was considered solely theoretical.

Perception accounts for the largest percentage of variability in a learner's processing of information. Interpretations of experiences can shape what is ultimately passed to short-term memory and on to long-term memory. Experiences in daily life help establish the environment in which children develop. The developmental process can be altered in various ways by the learner's interpretation of an experience. This plasticity during development enables individuals to integrate information gained through perception and advance to *knowing* from *not knowing*.

It was Piaget's view that from birth the human development process is programmed to change and that this change takes place in one direction at age-related intervals. Piaget explained that interpretations made by children from visual perceptions could chronicle their level (stage) of development.

During his investigations, Piaget posed questions in an oral context, while at other times a child might be shown diagrams and pictures. In either context, the child's response was one of perception and interpretation. Piaget explained that children faced with an experience would perceive the events and objects in keeping with their level of maturation. In other words, a ten-year-old would perceive and respond to an experience more in keeping with a knowledge of *concrete operations*. On the other hand, a five-year-old would have a more egocentric (self-centered) perception of objects and events in an experience.

Perception and interpretation are interrelated with experience. Developmentally, the plasticity of life means that the human condition can be shaped by experience.

Supported by theories of Piaget, Erikson, and Freud, John Dewey (1854–1952), education philosopher, proposed that schools should promote *freedom of experience* with few rules and restrictions (1897). At the same time, behaviorists were proposing that *the control of experience* was essential for learning new information and that learning could be measured by behavior (performance).

With human development comprised of the relationship between biology and our environment, according to the developmentalists, experience would be essential for the fulfillment of developmental stages. To enable an acquisition of knowledge, should the learner's experience be controlled or encouraged to interact freely?

PIAGET AND PERCEPTION

Generally speaking, it is therefore impossible to maintain that the concepts of intelligent thought are simply derived from the perceptions through abstraction and generalization. In addition to perceptual data, concepts incorporate specific instructions of a more or less complex nature. Logico-mathematical concepts presuppose a set of operations that are abstracted not from the objects perceived but from the actions performed on the objects, which is by no means the same. Even if every action can give rise to exteroceptive and proprioceptive perceptions, the schemes of these actions are no longer perceptible. In the case of physical concepts, etc., the proportion of perceptual information necessary is greater. However elementary they may be in the child, these concepts cannot be elaborated without a logico-mathematical structuration that, once again, goes beyond perception. (Piaget and Inhelder 1969, 49)

Piaget approached his work using a carefully designed system of observations. His studies were published from 1940 to 1970. Piaget's design for scientific study was not well accepted among psychologists at the time of its dissemination because behaviorism reigned in popularity.

An additional burden for Piaget's methods was that his early studies used his own children and qualitative methods. The field of educational research was preoccupied during that time with behaviorism and quantitative methods.

Nevertheless, there existed a group of followers among education practitioners who kept Piaget's work in the professional literature. His work can be described as observations of perception and performance and records of the child's perspective.

During the 1970s, when behaviorism was starting to wane, educators witnessed a return of interest to Piaget's work with an unusually large number of studies investigating his theories of perception among children (Nino 1979; Schiff and Saarni 1976; Nigl and Fishbein 1974; Borke 1971; Bower 1971).

Several important studies reported on the capacity of children to perceive and understand object relationships. An understanding of left/right perception, for example, is essential for reading comprehension in the United States, in which words flow from left to right on the printed page. Nigl and Fishbein (1974) explained a heuristic model for the developmental process in the coordination of tasks requiring that successful learners understand back/front, up/down, and left/right.

In the late 1960s, Sigel and Hooper (1968) compiled a series of articles in a single volume that explained (and, in most instances, validated) Piaget's explanations concerning *number concepts* as well as his *geometric* and *logical operations,* including *quantity, number,* and *weight.* The volume also included an important review of Piaget's famous *water-level perceptions* by young children.

From an infant study by Bower (1971), two important conclusions concerning perception were reported. First, during the course of infant development, infants seldom employ perceptual awareness of shape, size, and color in identifying objects prior to sixteen weeks of age.

Second, although they can perceive shape, size, and color features of objects, they do not employ this evidence to *identify* objects. Older infants, in contrast, use all of these identifying features in their perception of objects. This explanation would place *object permanence perceptions* occurring for some infants several months earlier than for children in Piaget's experiments.

Several studies have reported evidence at variance with Piaget's age-appointed stages of development (Gratch 1975). Some have inspired a query among U.S. parents about the feasibility of "training" their infants to achieve at or beyond Piaget's stages and thereby increase their opportunity to become "gifted" later in their youth. The response has been that the stages as explained by Piaget are a combination of biology and the environment, and they are invariant.

GESTALT PSYCHOLOGY AND LAWS OF PERCEPTION

Commonly described as a sum constituting more than the total of its equal parts, Gestaltism, in general, is made more understandable through a study of its theories of perception. Perceptual theories of Gestaltism are frequently credited to Max Wertheimer (1880–1943), Kurt Koffka (1886–1941), and Wolfgang Köhler (1887–1967), who were graduates of the University of Berlin and often referred to as the *Berlin Group.*

Piaget was aware of influences that the Berlin Group was having on the way his work was being evaluated in the scholarly community. Here, among other things, he suggests that perception does not have a role in intelligence when intelligence is properly defined.

To Piaget, intelligence was a product of the human development process—part environment and part biology. This view became steeped in the nature/nurture discussions. Piaget described his perspective on Gestaltism:

> Let us now turn to the operations themselves. . . . Max Wertheimer, one of the originators of Gestalt theory, has attempted to reduce them to perceptual structure. Gestaltism, as we know, interprets all intelligence as an extension, to wider and wider areas, of the "forms" initially governing the world of perceptions. What we have just said . . . contradicts such an interpretation. . . . It seems obvious, therefore, that operations, or intelligence in general, do not derive from the perceptual system. (Piaget and Inhelder 1969, 50)

The birth of Gestalt theories is often traced to Köhler's appointment in 1913 by the Prussian Academy of Science to director of the anthropoid station off the coast of the Canary Islands in Africa. Köhler spent four years at the station due to circumstances beyond his control. While there, he conducted scientific observations of apes and chickens. Taken primarily from observations of how apes solved problems, Köhler's *The Mentality of Apes* was published in 1917.

Köhler reported that apes employed *insight*. Here, insight is interchangeable with perception, in that their problem solving was not limited to trial and error. He thought it rather remarkable that apes solved problems through the use of mental capacities much like humans. The approach to understanding problem-solving behavior became basic to the study of Gestalt psychology and laws of perception that were refined by Wertheimer, Koffka, and Köhler to describe and demonstrate Gestalt theory.

Gestaltists are among the first to admit that the whole is composed of parts, and these parts and the whole can be understood through analysis. They point to numerous daily experiences that compromise our perception when a whole is converted into parts, and we are asked to convert these parts into their previous whole. An initial concern of Gestaltists, therefore, was to discover laws that govern our perception of wholes. Gestalt laws of perception were first described by Koffka (1935).

Gestalt Psychology and Laws of Perception

Gestalt psychology specifies four principles and one phenomenon: *principle of closure, principle of continuity, principle of similarity, principle of proximity,* and the *phi phenomenon.*

The principle of closure is the feeling one gets when the process of an act or pattern is complete (figure 3.1). In a visual field where one is presented with a series of forms that are incomplete in small details, memory of a similar form from a previous perceptual experience enables the perceiver to *fill in* the missing parts perceptually, and thereby bring *closure.* Psychologically, teachers can experience closure when poorly performing students improve their performance to an advanced level. From this experience, the teacher has a feeling of closing the student's failing state and advancing to a new level.

The principle of continuity is a perceptual experience that tends to interpret a line as continuous when it is presented in a pattern. A line passing through a series of similar shapes would make visible the straight line rather than a set of shapes (figure 3.2).

The principle of similarity is the perceptual phenomenon that interprets a relationship between objects that are similar. The principle of proximity suggests that human perceptual experiences tend to group similar objects.

Wertheimer's phi phenomenon is often perceived by an observer of a theater marquee displaying hundreds of flashing lights to attract pa-

Fig. 3.1   Incomplete forms perceived as complete from prior knowledge.

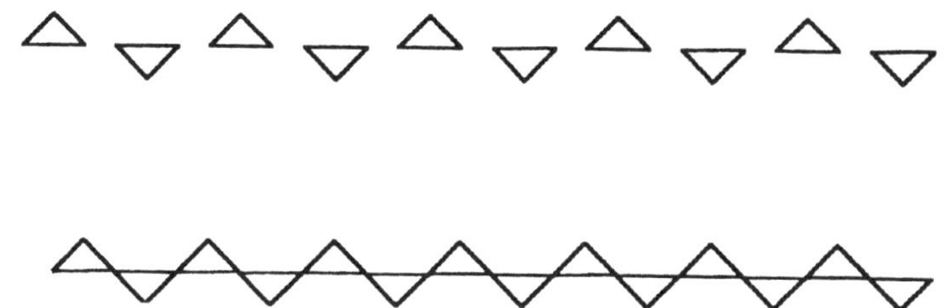

Fig. 3.2 A line passing through a series of similar shapes would make visible the straight line, rather than a set of shapes.

trons. In this regard, two or more flashing lights placed side by side do not appear to be separate lights but as lights that are moving.

Working with Wertheimer in theorizing Gestalt psychology from its early stages, Kurt Lewin departed significantly from those core elements of perception and memory that were commonly associated with Gestaltism, and placed an emphasis on *personality* and *motivation.*

Originally proposed by early Gestaltists, Lewin's model identified the field, figure, and ground as central to his concept of perception. These three elements of early Gestalt theory defined *field* as the perceived environment. Objects and events perceived within this field were labeled *figures*, and *ground* constituted the background. Individuals are unable to perceive figure and ground at the same time; however, figure and ground can alternate during a perceptual experience, or appear blended.

The picture in figure 3.3, for example, can be perceived as a vase or as faces in confrontation, but not both at the same time. As psychologists applied Lewin's interpretation of Gestalt, *field theory* was conceptualized beyond functional perception. Now, in the general field of psychology, Lewin's conceptualization of field has expanded Gestalt theory beyond the physical environment to include thoughtful (cognitive) initiatives like motives, goals, values, and associated social forces perceived to inhibit their fulfillment. The term *life space* was also introduced by Lewin and used to identify an expanded perception of field.

THE POWER OF SUBLIMINAL INFLUENCE

During the course of any school day, vast numbers of experiences occur in the lives of children and teachers that are interrelated during teach-

Fig. 3.3 Can be perceived as a vase or as faces in confrontation, but not both faces and vase at the same time.

ing and learning activities. How perceptions of these experiences affect learners and teachers will vary.

Students are asked by teachers to respond to selected experiences orally and in writing. Responses to such requests are often designed to encourage an advancement of knowledge for individual students.

Perceptions and variations in values and motives will determine the extent to which content will find its way into the student's long-term memory (learning).

Also, important chunks of knowledge will find their way into the student's memory through formal, but most probably informal, and unintentional transmissions. This form of information transfer is now referred to as the *hidden curriculum.*

The hidden curriculum implants information into the environment of schooling, including subtle references that are not easily discernible, but they are nonetheless introduced through interactions between children and school personnel.

Unintended messages can be transferred through the teacher's praise of selected behaviors, the teacher's body language, and other mannerisms that support values, morality, religious beliefs, patriotism, and etiquette, just to name a few.

These experiences are impossible to remove from schools and classrooms. It is therefore important for educators to be aware that their social status can be a powerful influence in the perceptions of students. This grants teachers, especially, an influence among students and their families, and grants privileges to educators that should be used with care, along with the awareness that their ideas and behaviors are directly influencing the perceptions of students.

Perception is the first step in shaping public ideas. If enough people are influenced to share ideas, such ideas can become *trends*. Trends in the hands of the politically powerful and socially influential can become public policy.

Theories of perception, like most other theories, range along a continuum. There are extreme views extending along the left expressing rather liberal views, suggesting free-flowing opportunities that the individual can enact based primarily upon values and open choices. These views are expressed in existentialism and phenomenology, each with the caveat that individuals must accept responsibility for what their perception unfolds (Zaner and Ihde 1973).

At the opposite end of the continuum, among others, are the Gestaltists. In their view, perception is primarily a function of vision. Here, there are specific principles that govern how we perceive our world. This rather conservative interpretation enables our choices *after* experiences are screened through established principles of perception.

Writing in 1978, Brownowski puts forth a view between these two extremes by suggesting that the human prerogative to select meaningful information from an experience is limited by what humans might *infer*.

> Perception of the senses is governed by mechanisms which make our knowledge of the outside world inferential. We do not receive impressions which are elemental. Our sense impressions are themselves constructed by the nervous system in such a way that they automatically carry with them an interpretation of what they see or hear or feel. (43)

PERCEPTION AND CLINICAL STUDIES

Three primary methods of gathering data on clients are used in clinical psychiatry and clinical psychology: case histories, psychological testing, and clinical observations. *Perception* is often a prominent feature in these studies. Perception in many instances has also been used to provide a theoretical framework for psychological tests in clinical work.

Psychological tests that have perception embedded in their theoretical framework have been used professionally at various times over the last hundred years. A group of instruments that can be associated with perception includes the *Rorschach Test,* the *Thematic Apperception Test* (TAT), and the *Myers-Briggs Type Indicator* (MBTI).

Clinicians have praised these instruments as very important, and at times even essential for their work. On the other hand, statisticians have been critical of their instrumental design and statistical analyses. Nevertheless, they remain in widespread use today, and are discussed here because of their reliance, in various ways, on perception in their theoretical implications and design.

The Rorschach instrument is made up of ambiguous patterns that appear to be derived from paper folded over an ink blot. For that reason, it has been commonly referred to as the "ink blot test" in popular media.

In administering the Rorschach Test, ambiguous ink blot patterns are presented on cards to the patient under study. After examining the cards, selected questions are asked of the patient with the intention of soliciting the patient's perceptual interpretation of each ambiguous pattern and separate parts (Beck 1937; Klopfer and Kelly 1942).

Ambiguity in the pictures is intentionally designed to encourage a response from the patient that is perceptually standardized from patient to patient. It is assumed by the clinician that individual responses reveal insights into a patient's personality, mental state, and under certain circumstances, even pathology.

Instruments like the Rorschach test can also be professionally reassuring to patients, especially when testing is followed with an interview that includes the patient's original complaint in the therapist's interpretation of their Rorschach responses or treatment plan (Wolberg,1967; DeCato and Piotrowski 1977).

The *Thematic Apperception Test* can consist of a series of pictures, a questionnaire, and/or interview. It was developed in the 1930s by H. A. Murray and has since been commonly called the *TAT*. The TAT, usually given in two sessions, is known as a projective test designed to attract the imagination of persons under study.

Here, the idea is that the patient will "project" ideas from their perceptions that could reveal underlying causes of pathologies, and thereby provide direction for clinical treatment. Typically, the patient is shown a picture that displays a typical social situation and asked something like "How do you think this situation came about?"

Patients are expected to reveal themes that are important in their lives. Interpretations are derived by attending clinicians from the patient's reflections, self-criticisms, and passive and/or aggressive oral responses. What the patient considers ideal (ideational content), the emergence of anxiety, and self-experiencing are perceptual responses that have significant values for the TAT clinician (Morgan and Murray 1935).

Based on the personality theory of Carl Gustav Jung (1915, 1921), the *Myers Briggs Type Indicator* (MBTI) is a paper-and-pencil-administered instrument with selected questions that are phrased in a manner that solicits perceptual responses to a series of behavioral statements.

Katherine C. Briggs and her daughter, Isabel Briggs Myers, developed the MBTI from their observations of personality types and cognitive styles (Myers and Briggs 1980).

From written responses to a standardized set of statements, the MBTI provides clinicians a scale that is scored semantically, with theoretically assigned behavioral and personality traits like *extroversion, introversion, sensing, judging, thinking,* and *feeling*.

Employed primarily by psychologists, counselors, and clerics, these labels are brought to the attention of the respondent, followed with recommendations for vocational, academic, friendship, and/or mate choices (Myers and McCaulley 1985).

FOUR

Acquiring Knowledge

Knowledge comes, but wisdom lingers.

—Alfred, Lord Tennyson

Learning as a word of science has specific meaning, but this specificity seldom occupies today's popular or professional interchanges. When information is stored as knowledge in long-term memory, it is learned—and the learned individual likely experiences changes in behavior as knowledge is increased.

When today's educators evaluate the degree to which a student has learned, more often than not, in reality they are quantifying *performance*. Such measurements do not evaluate the full extent to which learning has taken place. Test scores are at best indirect measures of individual performance; such scores do not inform the educator of the extent to which a person's performance actually matches what has been learned (memory). Educators commonly infer from a paper-and-pencil performance the extent to which learning has taken place. Such inferences do not, however, inform the examiner of the full extent to which knowledge has been acquired. It is also true that information is not the same as knowledge.

Working memory has a quality of integrating information gained from various experiences. The integration of previous information gained from past, present, and future experiences forms the foundation for knowledge acquisition.

To be placed in the sensory-neural system, information elicited from experience must first capture our attention. This information is then selectively processed by perception before being introduced to other areas in the processing network of the organism. The knowledge-acquisition process starts with experience and ends with working memory (long-term memory). Information in long-term memory, or working memory, is said to constitute learning.

Experience is accessible to individual receptive systems (visual, tactile, olfactory, auditory). Sensory systems enable a connection between the environment and our internal neural systems. The major component in this system is the neuron. The system is the human central nervous system (CNS).

THE HUMAN NEURAL SYSTEM: HISTORICAL PERSPECTIVES

During the late 1800s, philosophers in England and Germany were looking to psychology as the area of discourse from which a theory of logic could emerge. Following some separations between psychology and philosophy, some scholars who elected to pursue psychology as a discipline of choice worked toward gaining the acceptance of psychology as a science.

Psychologists were creating their separation from philosophy by applying the rigors of the scientific method to complex problems of logic. This period of advanced thought in philosophy and psychology has been identified by various scholars as the emergence of psychology as a science and termed *psychologism*. Not all scholars of psychology accepted the new "scientific" identities; philosophy remained an area of logical thought that could neither be proved nor disproved.

One of the critics disdainful of psychology as a science was Ivan Petrovich Pavlov (1849–1936). As a professor of pharmacology and physiology, he received the Nobel Prize in 1904 for his laboratory work on the digestive system. Psychologists, especially John B. Watson in the United States, embraced Pavlov's work with classical conditioning. Late in life, he started serious study of classical conditioning but was reported to have reprimanded any lab assistant who referred to his work as psychology or psychologism.

Also during the late 1800s, following the trends of scientific models in psychology, Sigmund Freud pursued an interdisciplinary study of information acquisition by humans. Freud wrote to his close friend and ally, Wilhelm Fleiss, about his work on a *Project for Scientific Psychology* to delineate a comprehensive study of a physiological, anatomical, and neural function of the human information system, and how they related to the brain in conscious deliberations (Freud 1954).

Freud sought an understanding of the objective transmission of information by the human organism, which he thought would lead to a clearer understanding of the objective categories of psychopathology. Fleiss was not only unimpressed, he suggested that Freud stop wasting his time and abandon the project.

With little assistance from his friend and colleague, Freud could not resolve the serious dilemma with which he was confronted. Freud's dilemma came from a confusion of the manner in which the brain, after receiving an impulse traveling through the central nervous system, could simultaneously be available to continuous sensations like hunger and sex on the same "track." Freud pondered the need for a single system of transmission along the human neural pathway from the senses to the brain, when more than a single sensation was being transmitted. When a response was required, Freud thought sensations traveled in both directions. These questions were posed in his 1895 notes.

> From the very first, however, the principle of inertia is upset by another set of circumstances. As the internal complexity of the organism increases, the neuronic system receives stimuli from the somatic element itself—endogenous stimuli, which calls forth for discharge. These have their origin in the cells of the body and give rise to the major needs: hunger, respiration, and sexuality. The organism cannot withdraw itself from them as it does from external stimuli; it cannot employ their quantity (Q) for the purpose of flight from the stimuli. They only cease if certain definite conditions are realized in the external world. (Take, for example, the case of the need for nourishment.) To carry out an action (that will bring these conditions about)—an action which deserves to be called "specific"—requires an effort which is independent of endogenous quantities and is generally greater than they are, since the individual is placed under conditions which may be described as "the exigencies of life." The neuronic system is consequently obliged to abandon its original trend towards inertia (than is, towards a reduction of its level of tension to zero). It must learn to tolerate a store of quantity sufficient to meet the demands for specific action. In so far as it does so, however, the same trend will persist in the modified form of a tendency to keep the quantity down, at least, so

far as possible and avoid any increase in it (that is, to keep its level of tension constant). All the performances of the neuronic system are to be comprised under the heading either of the primary function or of the secondary function imposed by the exigencies of life. (Freud 1954, 357–58)

This particular problem ultimately led to Freud's abandonment of his scientific project. Ideas about learning, thought, and higher mental processes are now theorized around the central nervous system (sometimes referred to as the *conceptual nervous system*). Though the labels might vary somewhat, and the term *synapse* was not introduced until 1897, Freud's description of the human nervous system is surprisingly similar to the model described in university textbooks today.

The essence of this new knowledge that the neuronic system consists of dystinct [*sic*] but similarly constructed neurons which only have contact with one another through an intervening foreign substance and which terminate on one another in the same manner as on a piece of foreign tissue; that certain lines of conduction are laid down on them, in so far as they receive excitations through a cell process (or dendrite) and discharge them through an axis cylinder (or axone); and furthermore, that they have numerous ramifications and diameters of various dimensions. . . . The structure of the neurone makes it possible that these resistances are in the contacts (between the neurones) which thus function as *barriers*. (Freud 1954, 358)

CLASSICAL AND TRADITIONAL BEHAVIORISM

Introduced in the United States in the 1920s, behavioristic studies employing animals and humans provided the major context for investigations of the acquisition of knowledge. By the late 1950s, behaviorism still prevailed; however, variations away from classical behavioral approaches were starting to emerge. First introduced by Ivan Pavlov, and promoted in the United States by John B. Watson, classical conditioning was criticized by B. F. Skinner as being too limiting.

Classical conditioning as explained through the work of Pavlov and Watson dealt with individual responses to stimuli. Here, stimuli would be introduced by the examiner to promote a desired response (negative or positive). It was noted that positive responses following an act would entice the responder to repeat that act. This pattern was called *stimulus response (S/R)* because of its simplistic structure of shaping behavior that resulted from the pairing of a stimulus with a desired behavior (Watson 1930).

Skinner supported the general concepts of behaviorism but took a broader view. Skinner described attention as the most important phase of learning, and that future attending could be shaped by reinforcement. Skinner explained that stimulus and behavior was more complex among humans than what was described in the S/R model. Further, a human response frequently does not result from an obvious (selected or assumed) stimulus.

Skinner labeled responses that flow from a stimulus *respondents*; responses that flow from the organism were labeled *operants*. In this model, operant behavior acts *on* the environment and respondent behavior reacts *to* the environment. The most important human behavior, according to Skinner, was *operant*. This model is based somewhat on a principle that is believed by many professionals and the general population that humans behave in a manner that avoids pain and that they are attracted to pleasure.

Negative Reinforcement

In an experiment that presents a puppy being fed while housed in a screened-in cage, the puppy starts to wag his tail in delight. As soon as the tail wagging starts, the attendant stops the flow of food. The flow of food starts again when the puppy stops wagging his tail. It is theorized that after a few episodes of eating-wagging-stopping of food, the puppy will be reluctant to repeat the tail wagging.

Positive Reinforcement

A puppy is placed in a similar screened cage and not fed for several hours. Mounted in the cage is a small screened box that contains food. The food can be seen but is not easily accessible. When the puppy becomes hungry, he starts to scratch at the screened walls of the cage and the screened box containing food. After several trials, the puppy accidentally hits the lever that releases food. After consuming the first tasty portion, it is likely that the puppy will repeat the behavior that produced the first morsel.

Reinforcement

Within the framework of positive and negative reinforcement, Skinner described reinforcement as *primary* and *general*. Skinner's primary sources of reinforcements are borrowed from behaviors described by Freud and earlier psychologists as *drives*, often erroneously referred to as *instincts*. They include food, water, reproductive activity, and physical stability. General reinforcements are stimuli that are not reinforcing but can become reinforcing when paired with *primary reinforcement*. For example, a soft carpet can be placed in the dog cage (mentioned in the positive reinforcement example) after eating is complete. Here, the soft carpet, when paired with the food (primary reinforcer), would become a positive reinforcer, which it would not be in the absence of feeding.

The most frequently identified concepts among Skinner's ideas that are borrowed by educators are *extinction* and *forgetting*. In present-day testing environments, this has become a major focus of classroom teachers. In many school districts, teachers are partially or completely held accountable for their students to demonstrate on a written test that they have not forgotten what has been taught (Linn, Baker, and Betebenner 2002).

According to Skinner, extinction often occurs in an experimental context similar to the two previously cited. After such an induced reinforcing experience, in the cases cited, an animal will discontinue the behavior elicited by reinforcement. This can also occur when the subject in the experiment is a human. On the other hand, forgetting is a much slower process but produces the same results as extinction not resulting from reinforcement. Forgetting occurs naturally after a passage of time. Chapter 6 explores a fuller view of forgetting.

The field of psychology in the 1950s and '60s had no shortage of behaviorists conducting human and animal experiments and proposing variations on the basic principles of classical conditioning. An important voice that brought additional attention to the work of Pavlov, Watson, and Skinner was that of Edwin R. Guthrie (1886–1959).

Guthrie, a graduate of the University of Nebraska, studied philosophy and mathematics (psychology as a field of study was still in its infancy during Guthrie's university experience), but he shifted to a concentration in behavioral psychology after receiving a Ph.D. in philosophy from the University of Pennsylvania. Guthrie's major influences came from the work of John B. Watson. This led to his work that was based upon behavioristic thought common in the 1930s (Guthrie 1935).

Over the years, Guthrie's work, though considered significant by many, remained mostly overshadowed by the more well-known Watson and Skinner. Guthrie's explanations of knowledge acquisition were different from those of prevailing psychology of the time, and are viewed by many to be more applicable to teaching and classroom learning.

Guthrie theorized that combinations of stimuli, or a single stimulus that has been proven to produce a response, render a similar response if the stimulus or stimuli are repeated. He referred to stimuli as *habits* or *bonds*. Guthrie cited three methods for breaking habits or bonds, and thereby replacing undesirable habits with desirable ones.

Flooding is a technique of presenting stimuli repeatedly to provoke a repetition of the undesirable response. Eventually, the organism will become fatigued with the behavior and can no longer respond in the undesirable manner. Fatigue will set in and the organism will change the behavior or refrain from all behaviors. The most recent response will replace the undesirable one(s).

Incompatible stimuli means that the stimuli are presented with a new choice when the undesirable response is unavailable. In this regard, a new response must be selected as a target in place of the old stimuli.

The *threshold method* presents the stimulation in a subdued form when the stimulus is too weak to elicit the old (undesirable) response. This probably elicits a different response, which can then be increased gradually until this more desirable response is strengthened enough to replace the original undesirable one.

THE BLENDING OF BEHAVIORISM

Donald Olding Hebb (1904–1985) can be credited with creating a bridge between behaviorism and higher mental functions. He brought to the field of psychology stimulus-response models but gradually made the transition to higher human mental functions, thus creating a role for the human central nervous system (1949).

Born in Nova Scotia, and attending their schools until receiving a B.A. degree from Dalhousie University, Hebb completed a master's degree at the University of Chicago and a Ph.D. in psychology at Harvard.

Hebb served as editor of the *Bulletin of the Canadian Psychological Association* where he also served as its president, as well as president of the American Psychological Association. He authored many papers, as well as a textbook published in three editions, which remains in use today.

In part, these influential positions in psychology enabled him to exert a considerable amount of influence toward loosening the grip that traditional behaviorism had on the field of psychology. William James, in 1898, had also proposed that learning (memory) was probably not a single system, as behaviorists were theorizing (Watson 1930; Skinner 1953).

Often referred to as the founder of cognitive psychology, Hebb's writings also include *A Neuropsychological Theory* (1959), *The Organization of Behavior* (1949), and *A Textbook on Psychology* (1958, 1966, 1972).

Hebb accepted the S/R concept in its general formulation but was critical of what traditional behaviorists explained as a direct, almost immediate or relatively short, duration time between stimulus and response. The time between *S* and *R* varied somewhat among the different theorists until Hebb; even in Hebb's view, however, this separation in time between *S* and *R* remained modest.

Hebb explained that the time between stimulus and response involved in knowledge acquisition allowed for a higher mental process. During these mental processes, Hebb explained that there was probably a role for *S/R*, but that role did not completely account for the variety of steps in the acquisition of knowledge.

This time delay left a lot to be desired from the unitary *S/R* model. Hebb explained that perception and thinking should occupy some time between *S* and *R*. In this regard, he viewed psychology as a biological science. This was followed by his neuropsychological cell-assembly construct (Hebb 1949; Milner 1957).

Hebb also explained that the brain used two separate neural mechanisms, with a short-term storage that he called a *primary mechanism* and a long-term mechanism that reflected neuronal links between assemblies of cells (Craik and Lockhart 1972; Melton 1963).

This book, in part, is compatible with Hebb's theory in suggesting that acquisition of knowledge involves *experience, attention, perception,* and *memory,* with *retrieval* as a response.

Presented here is a current model of information processing by the central nervous system that is built upon ideas introduced through Hebb's work (1972).

LEARNING STYLES: AN IDEA IN SEARCH OF A THEORY

Learning styles is a popular idea that surfaced in the 1970s. The popularization of learning styles has been due in part to the unusual number of doctoral dissertations that have examined this topic. Many early studies that identified learning styles as their major interest, actually cited cognitive styles in their reference lists without noting in the text that cognitive styles were grounded in personality studies dating from the 1930s and did not confirm learning styles (Allport, 1937).

Some positive results were achieved by teachers who were early adherents to learning style ideas because the topic brought to the attention of teachers that there is great variety among learners. Even though learner variability was known at the time, teachers now had published materials to support their recognition of students who approached their work in ways that were different. Among other things, learning styles encouraged teachers to try different methods when children did not, or could not, perform well academically (Dunn & Dunn, 1978).

Results varied for teachers who modified their practice with an infusion of their own brand of learning styles. But many teachers embraced the idea that when children failed in the classroom, it might be the manner in which material was presented and the child's preferences for engagement, rather than the intellectual capacity of the child. This book makes similar observations, but identifies attending and perception, rather than learning style, as the reason for learner variation in memory and retrieval (figure 5.1).

Still others in the field suggested that when desirable performance scores occurred among school children being studied, it was not the result of matching the "styles" of students with the "styles" of their teachers; but from the fact that slow learners, after getting extra attention of any sort, were motivated to try harder. Whatever the reasons for some positive results, many in the education research community were generally skeptical of the theoretical foundations of learning styles, and the use of "learning" in its label.

By the 1990s, when the fields of education and psychology became overwhelmed with the large number of published papers on learning styles, studies started to appear in research literature that were critical of the idea. Following the learning-style work of Kolb (1985), for example, more than 700 scholarly papers citing his works were published (Lawson & Johnson, 2002).

In the early 1980s, Richard Riding was a leading contributor to the research literature on learning styles. By the 1990s, Riding's contributions on the subject separated the concept of learning styles from cognitive styles, and discussed the descriptors as two different concepts (Rayner, S., & Riding, R., 1997). By 2003, Riding and associates avoided ideas of learning styles, and were paring studies of cognitive styles with working memory (Riding, J., Grimley, M., Dahraei, H., & Banner, G., 2003).

Kolb's learning styles construct is reportedly based on theories of personality first developed by C. G. Jung. The Myers-Briggs Type Indicator (MBTI), a cognitive styles instrument is also based on the work of Jung (Morgan, 1997). It is within the theoretical framework of Jung and Myers-Briggs that foundations for Kolb's learning styles constructs were developed (Kolb, 1976, 1984). And, this aspect of Kolb's work has been viewed with extensive skepticism (Freedman R. D., & Stumpf, S. A., 1978; Freedman, R. D., & Stumpf, S. A., 1980).

The Kolb learning style dimensions are identified as perceiving and processing within two bipolar domains; concrete-abstract, and active-reflective. These two domains are integrated into framing four learning styles; divergent, convergent, assimilating, and accommodating. The categories used to identify Kolb's learning styles are:

1. Divergent learners perceive information concretely and process it reflectively.
2. Convergent learners perceive information abstractly and process it reflectively.
3. Assimilating learners perceive information abstractly, and process it actively.
4. Accommodating learners perceive information concretely and process it actively. (Kolb, 1976, 1984) (Emphasis added)

The reader should note the extent to which perceiving occupies a major role in each of Kolb's learning styles descriptors. Refer to figure 5.1 and recognize that perception is level one (1) of the learning process; therefore, does not constitute the whole of learning. This single level can render itself to individualistic styles, but learning occupies all four (4) levels, rendering the domain referred to as learning styles doubtful at best.

From their studies, Lawson and Johnson (2002) reported that Kolb's learning styles lacked validity and predictive value and therefore had serious theoretical flaws. Garner (2000), Reynolds (1997), and Cronwell & Manfredo (1994), made similar reports.

THE NEUROSCIENCE OF LANGUAGE ACQUISITION

Approximately fifty years ago, Noam Chomsky proposed a theory of language acquisition that required innate neural qualities. Chomsky theorized that humans, at birth, possessed neural tracts in their brain that are intentionally specialized to process language (1965, 1968).

Possibly, Chomsky's theory introduces the idea of a single human instinct that might exist in our human potential for acquiring language, now commonly detailed as a *language acquisition device (LAD)*. LAD proposes that, at birth, children possess the innate capacity, with intention, to learn a language (Pinker 1994). This phenomenon appears to be true for all children in all cultures, regardless of the complexities in the language of their parents (Lenneberg 1967).

Biologically, the language acquisition device is not specific to the child's capacity to learn a particular language, such as English, for example. For this reason, and because of various aspects regarding how this innate capacity is structured, different ideas are being proposed as of this writing; this has the potential to bring clarity to this complex concept in the near future (Bohannan, MacWinney, and Snow 1990; Morgan 1990; Ritchie and Bhatia 1999; just to name a few).

THE CENTRAL NERVOUS SYSTEM (CNS)

After information from experience and attention is successfully selected by perception, it becomes a likely candidate to enter the individual's short-term and then long-term memory. Long-term memory is stored in the brain. The human brain consists of layers called *laminae* and rounded structures called *nuclei*. These layers and structures are designed to carry out a series of complex functions involving networks that require large numbers of neurons. It is surprising that the nature and function of the neuron, the center of information processing in the human conceptual system, is rarely written about or discussed by education scholars.

Information is carried from the experience to the brain by a system of communication and control called the *human nervous system.* This complex labyrinth starts with the *neuron.* Neurons receive and send information as impulses. The human nervous system is built upon the neuron as its primary structure in sending and receiving information. The central nervous system is comprised of neurons in the brain and spinal cord.

A neuron is composed of a cell body and its extensions. Figure 4.2 is a diagram of a neuron, synapses, and their circuits. Found on all sides of the nerve cell are thin microscopic *dendrites* (A). Dendrites carry impulses toward the cell body. The *axon,* a thick extension, carries impulses away from the cell body.

The end of each axon is extremely close to the dendrites of the next neuron, but they do not touch. A microscopic gap exists between the axon of one neuron, and the dendrite of the adjoining neuron. This gap is called a *synapse* (B). Even though they do not actually touch at the synapse, the gap is tiny enough to allow chemical signals to pass between the nerve cells. These chemical signals are called *neurotransmitters.* A neurotransmitter is the substance released at the nerve endings when transmitting an impulse to a neuron, a gland, or a muscle.

Nerve cells contain an equal number of ions (positively or negatively charged atoms). Chemical and electrical charges are involved in the movement of nerve impulses (information) through individual nerve cells. Prior to the transmission of information by a neuron, its outside layer is composed of electrically charged positive sodium ions. Its inside layer is composed of electrically charged negative potassium ions. When the neuron is transmitting, the sodium and the potassium ions change places.

In their new positions, the outside of the nerve cell becomes negative and the inside becomes positive. After the impulse has passed through the nerve cell, the sodium and potassium ions return to their original places. These changes occur in every segment of the cell as information passes through the neuron (Fig. 4.1).

This arrangement ensures that information is *invariant* (does not vary) in the direction of travel. Information sent from experiences involving the hand is sent to the brain in the same chemical/electrical pattern previously stated as impulses that are ocular, for example.

Information from different sensory sources, however, are received and processed in different areas of the brain. The brain translates these as different types of experiences and some require a response. Motor responses are translated through the peripheral nervous system (PNS).

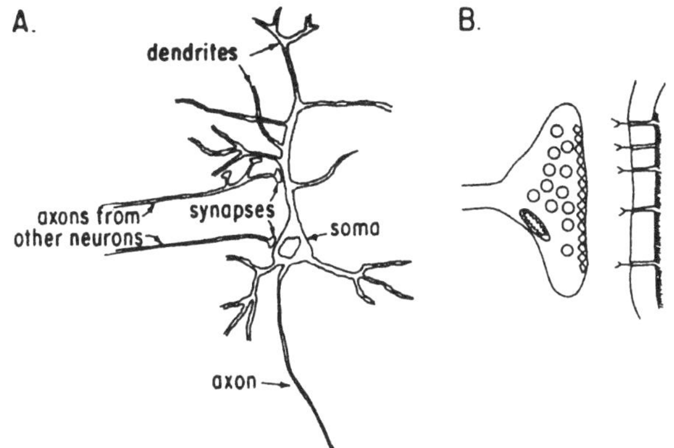

Fig. 4.1   Neurons in circuits and synapses.

THE PERIPHERAL NERVOUS SYSTEM (PNS)

The central nervous system, consisting of neurons in the brain and spinal cord, is one of two parts of the human nervous system. The other part, the peripheral nervous system, is composed of forty-three pairs of nerves leading from the brain and spinal cord to other parts of the body. Impulses transmitted through the peripheral nervous system require a response.

In this regard, impulses are transmitted through motor neurons back to the area from where the information originated. Depending upon the nature of the experience, motor neurons stimulate glands or muscles to respond to, or interact in, a particular experience.

For example, contemplate the tremendous amount of information that must be processed by an athlete during an experience called a *game*: During an important basketball game, the score is tied. In the last minutes of play, the rapidly unfolding experiences of the game, the excited players, and a boisterous audience find the player with the ball processing a tremendous amount of information. This rapidly changing experience has engaged the central nervous system (CNS) and the peripheral nervous system (PNS) of each individual involved in this experience. The player in possession of the ball is processing information about the position of each player on the court, information about those who are not moving and those who are, where their present movement is likely to take each of them, and in what amount of time. In addition to this tremendous flow of information engaging the CNS, thoughtful responses from each player are necessary. For the player with the ball now, her or his PNS will transmit impulses to muscles or glands that inform when to pass to one of four other players, to dribble closer to the target, or make an attempt to score immediately, or later. The CNS will also transmit information about how to identify our team/their team (color of uniform?). Choices must be made in the CNS and PNS practically in milliseconds. Information processing (CNS) and motor responses (PNS) are being called upon simultaneously. The quality of player performance during this information-processing episode separates exceptional players from players who perform less well.

Children have skills available to them in some environments, and during certain experiences, that might not be available to them under different circumstances. It is common to hear teachers describe the in-classroom behaviors of boys as moving about at their desks, interrupting others with their twisting and turning about.

This style of behavior is desirable during an athletic game and in a gymnasium, but is usually suppressed in the classroom. Some girls and boys have intellectual capacities available to them in active environments that might not be available to them in the passive environment of the testing center or classroom.

The processing of information is, in a manner of speaking, the same during *active* experiences as it is during *passive* experiences. We are familiar with the usual outward appearance of information processing during passive experiences (remaining seated and quietly attending to paper-and-pencil schoolwork). The last vignette described the processing of information during an active experience.

Despite the common perception of sportswomen and men as inarticulate "jocks" with modest intellectual capacity, we must dispel that myth as an inaccurate assessment of a highly intellectual, functioning group of people. The most accomplished athletes are successful because they have the capacity to process a tremendous amount of information, often in an inordinately small physical space, and in a short period of time.

ACTION AND COGNITION

In examining the coordinating elements of visual motor coordination and neural participation in the multiple processes involved in the *game*, a starting point could be the work in neuroscience with the notion of two visual systems. The idea that humans utilize two neural pathways in object relations has been studied in neuroscience for more than fifty years (Apter 1946; Polyak 1957). Many theories of human development start with studies of lesions in humans and induced conditions in animals. Theories of human vision and its relationship to motor systems have followed these pathways. Studies of cognition, movement, and motor response have included kittens (Hein and Held 1967), monkeys (Jeannerod 1973; Cowey and Stoerig 1995), and rodents (Goodale 1983). From these studies, the field of cognitive neuroscience has learned a great deal about human performance from which educators can also benefit.

The prefrontal cortex of the brain and memory are central to understanding planning and action. In the *game*, there are obvious motor actions involving the hand and object manipulation as interaction between self and object. This process also involves object identification and visual targets, which introduces what we know about visuomotor theory and development.

We have knowledge about many primitive associations between the hand and grasping behaviors. We have the results of studies related to a precision grip (pencil, scalpel), a grip for power (bat, hammer), or a grip for control (tennis racket, football, basketball). We know that grips differ in part by the position of the fingers and thumb—sometimes supporting, sometimes in opposition (Napier 1961; Heffner and Masterton 1975; Christel 1993). We also know that in the game, positions and actions of the hand and fingers are controlled through communication and coordination, all shaped by neurons within the brain and central nervous system.

ACTION AND CHILD DEVELOPMENT

The prefrontal cortex of the brain is central to the human capacity for planning. Piaget combined two human capacities; sensory (the senses) and motor (action and movement) to describe an early stage of development that he named the *sensorimotor* stage. Foundations for sensorimotor capacities are framed between eighteen and thirty-six months. Here, for an appreciation of the idea of *action* and *cognition*, educators should start with concepts of *sensorimotor development* first theorized by Piaget.

Piaget identified the sensorimotor period as extending from twelve to eighteen months. During this period, human capacities are developed for memory, planning, and action. Piaget suggested that sensorimotor capacities are developed during childhood experiences in the early years. It is therefore essential that children remain free to expand their experiences in a safe and trusting environment.

For example, different sensorimotor capacities can be expected from children who are confined to a four-by-six playpen for long hours during their early development when these children with such restrictive experiences are compared at a later age with children who experienced this same developmental period with the freedom to wander about their home less restricted.

During this sensorimotor period of exploration, children can have new and exciting discoveries while sometimes having minor mishaps that contribute to their experiences with minor bumps and bruises. Piaget has identified this period as one of *development through discovery*, where such things as mathematical concepts are first reasoned by the young.

In addition to the actual participation in sensorimotor activities, memory traces and repeatable experiences are rehearsed in the neural systems. It has been reported that images recorded in memory through imagining can have the same effect as if the individual actually carried out the act itself (Farah 1989; Fadiga et al. 1995). For this concept to be fully effective in expanding individual knowledge, the content being imaged should have laid down traces from actual earlier experiences. In this case, what is being imagined has connections with earlier experiences.

FIVE

Memory

> Remember thee!
>
> Ay, thou poor ghost, while memory holds a seat in this distracted globe. Remember thee! Yea, from the table of my memory I'll wipe away all trivial fond records, all saws of books, all forms, all pressures past, that youth and observations copied there.
>
> —William Shakespeare, *Hamlet*

In cognitive neuroscience, memory is defined as a trio of human events: encoding, storage, and retrieval. *Encoding* includes experience and perception, and *storage* includes sensory, short-term, and long-term store. *Retrieval* is demonstrated through individual performance with memory as a source (and covered further in chapter 6).

References to memory can be traced to ancient times. Perhaps the earliest references to memory can be found in fables that were memorized and told to others by a black slave, Aesop. He is reported to have been born in Phrygia, Asia Minor. In his day, he was called Ethiop (for Ethiopian), and more recent literature has referred to him as a philosopher and Negro slave (Eliot 1909; Snowden 1970).

Aesop lived around 560 B.C.E., more than 500 years before the birth of Christ, and almost 1,000 years before Aristotle, Socrates, and Plato were active as scholars. Socrates spent his final days putting Aesop's fables to verse (Rogers 1972).

During the time of Aesop, storytelling was an art, and good storytellers were referred to as *prophets*. Prophets were individuals who traveled among the various towns, encampments, and gatherings, sharing news from groups they had previously visited. Prophets passed on information that aided groups in their awareness that, within travel distance, there were others like them.

The best or most popular prophets embedded their news in interesting tales, and their visits were anticipated with greater expectation than the average fablers.

Occasionally, after hearing a tale, villagers would actually experience or recall similar events from their experiences and conclude that good prophets must have supernatural powers. What followed was their desire to communicate with strangers through weaving their own stories (fables) from memory. Aesop's fables were memorized and retold by various prophets thousands of times (Eliot 1909).

Aesop was the most celebrated among the prophets, and his news (fables) was memorized and translated into many different languages. Aesop's fables were used to disseminate his philosophy. Appearing in many languages, his fables described concepts such as honesty, compassion, justice, and virtue, just to name a few.

As an academic exercise during the time of Socrates, Aristotle, and Plato, school children were given Aesop's fables to translate into different languages. Many believe that because of translation exercises during their early schooling, the work of many Greek philosophers reflected ideas originally expressed in the memorized fables of Aesop (Rogers 1972; Snowden 1970).

For ancient history, European and U.S. scholars seldom investigate the works of African and Asian scholars. Their attention is directed to Italian and Greek philosophers, and their university courses are called *Western Civilization*. This eliminates attention to non-European scholars who were active centuries earlier. Memory today is encouraged from exposure to schooling, TV, readings, and so forth—but far too often, false histories or limited histories are established in our memories.

> By the time Alexander was sweeping the civilized world with conquest after conquest from Chaeronia to Gaza; from Babylon to Cabul; by the time the first Aryan conquerors were learning the rudiments of the war and government at the feet of philosophic Aristotle; and by the time Athens was laying down the foundations of modern European civilization, the earliest and greatest Ethiopian culture had already flourished and dominated the civilized world for over four centuries and a half. (Danquah 1927, 3)

Even the general public is familiar with Aesop's fables because they are often recited as moral "lessons" in public conversations. Moral statements like "A wolf in sheep's clothing," for example, follows one of Aesop's fables.

Memory is a basic concept in the fable *The Nightingale and the Swallow*:

> A swallow, conversing with a nightingale, advised her to leave the leafy grove where she had made her home, and to come and live with men, nesting under the shelter of their roofs, as she herself did. But the nightingale replied, "There was a time when I lived among men, as do you, but the *memory* of the cruelties that I suffered at their hands is so strong that never again will I come near their dwellings."
>
> The moral: *The scene of past suffering renews painful memories.* (Emphasis added.)

Aesop's awareness of memory as a conscious recall of a previous experience was probably not separated from other thoughts because in a world where reading and interpreting from symbols was not common, speaking from things remembered was necessary.

In societies where the spoken word, rather than the written word, was the primary means of transferring information, stories, tales, and fables would vary greatly from retelling.

Ribot (1882) was among the early medical writers who focused on the nature of memory as a *remembrance,* and the acceptance of an individual's interpretation of a remembrance, as was common during the time of Aesop, represents a precursor of phenomenology (Reiff and Scheerer 1959). See chapter 3 for an extensive discussion of phenomenology.

It might be difficult for some to imagine that there was a time without telephones, radios, TVs, and the Internet; that lapse in our memory is understandable. It is equally remarkable, however, that given today's plethora of communication instruments, and in the most powerful country in the world, as many as 30 percent of U.S. citizens cannot read or write—yet in the small country of Cuba, almost 100 percent of the citizens can read.

Because information is laid down in neural tracts, means of communication—like writing letters or reading books—are significant instruments of information collection for those who can read.

By the 1970s, memory as a human sensory function was being described in two domains: *semantic* memory and *episodic* memory (Tulving 1992; Altmann and John 1999). Episodic memory flows from the perception of an experience that can be defined as an episode. Perceptions of memory from other experiences are called *semantic memory*. Human semantic memory is extensive, in that it encompasses most of what we know about the universe.

In the 1980s, because of an increase in clinical studies, the identification of memory into two domains was advanced to two memory systems, primarily for the study of amnesia, during which one system is thought to be impaired while the other remains relatively normal (Cermak 1982; Jacoby and Witherspoon 1982).

Hebb proposed a dual memory system that involved reverberating neural circuits that acted to change chemical reactions to synaptic junctures where long-term memory is created (Christianson 1992; Cahill and McGaugh 1996; McGaugh and Herz 1972). During the 1970s and '80s, studies concentrated on conscious retrieval strategies for episodes and experiences stored in long-term memory.

By the 1990s, Schacter and others embarked on studies of *implicit* and *explicit* memory. This followed an emerging interest in memory traces remaining from subconscious remembrances called *implicit memory*. It is presumed that remembrances of episodes are not required for implicit memory. Explicit memory, on the other hand, requires a conscious remembrance from an observed experience (Roediger 1990; Buckner et al. 1995; Schacter and Buckner 1998).

The important thing for teachers to know here is that the implicit/explicit theory is suggesting that a lesson (experience) can lay down memory traces of an explicit experience that are not necessarily retrievable; however, the current experience (lesson) can evoke remembrances of an earlier experience in the student's thoughts (implicit). When the two experiences are brought together in the student's thinking, a Gestalt awareness can emerge as an "ah-ha" (Gabrieli et al. 1995).

There is a controversy among clinical scholars over a dual memory system comprised of procedural matters and reflection versus a single long-term memory system (Moscovitch 1982). Because a further discussion of this clinical controversy is of minor utility for our readers toward an understanding of human memory, the disagreement among clinical scholars concerning these details will not be advanced here (Gobet 2000b).

HISTORICAL PERSPECTIVES

Hermann Ebbinghaus (1885), an early empiricist, was among the first to *scientifically* study human memory and its retention. W. B. Pillsbury, writing in the late 1800s, followed the Ebbinghaus empirical traditions in his study of perception. Also, studies from the early 1900s divided memory into a subcategory called *selective memory.*

Influenced by the scientific measurement theory of Fechner, Ebbinghaus elected to apply Fechner's method (1860) to his study of memory. In the late 1800s, there were few problems related to developing a scientific paper describing ideas about memory from a philosophical perspective. For this approach, one would not need supportive empirical data.

Given the state of science rapidly emerging in the early 1900s, however, it is unlikely that studies could gain much acceptance in the scientific community without empirical support. Therefore, it must have been a major discovery for Ebbinghaus to stumble upon Fechner's *Elements of Psychophysics* in a secondhand bookstore in Paris. In this find, Ebbinghaus uncovered an application of an experimental method appropriate for his study of memory (Baddeley 1976).

From a functional perspective, models that describe and display cognitive processing do so from descriptions of various labels for memory, which are then defined as learning. More often than not, memory categories in scholarly literature follow variations on the Atkinson and Shiffrin model (1968). A model representing theories of Broadbent (1958), Atkinson and Shiffrin (1968), and Baddeley (1998) are represented in figure 5.1.

The first stage is usually storage for a brief sensory input, *sensory store*, which originally did not include what is generally thought of as memory. This is followed by a short-term store, which in recent scientific literature has been referred to as *working memory* (Baddeley 1999; Ericsson and Kintsch 2000), and finally for long-term store (what has been learned).

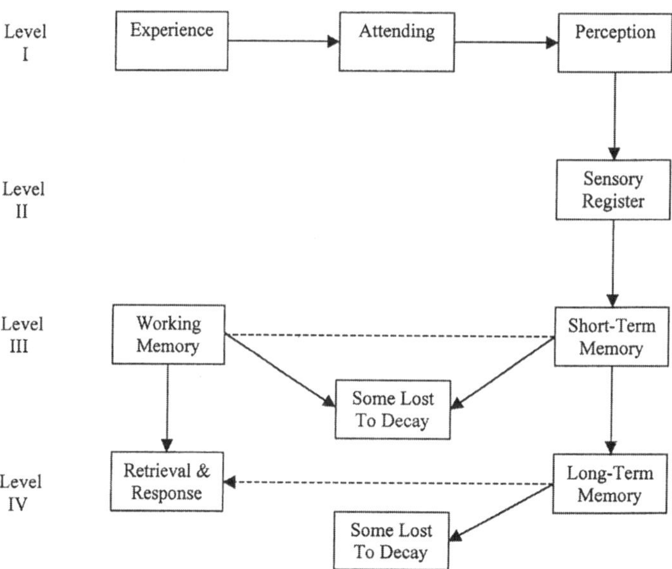

Fig. 5.1   A model of information processing.

Working memory is employed in cognitive processing to expand human learning capacities through reasoning and comprehension. As of this writing, working memory is thought to have a limited capacity for performing information processing tasks. Investigators have also suggested that working memory is responsible for storage and information processing. A limited capacity for working memory is created in part by this dual role, thereby increasing its vulnerability to decay (figure 4.1)

In essence, recent studies suggest that new information received from experiences is held in working memory for brief periods of time until the organism can determine the meaning of this new input. Despite an almost common agreement concerning the short retention span for working memory, some investigators have associated working memory with long-term memory (Morris & Jones, 1990; Ericsson & Kintsch, 1995, 2000).

Studies report that working memory has three important features; the central executive, a phonological loop and a visuo-spatial sketch pad. The central executive controls and integrates information from the two latter domains. The phonological loop stores verbal information for short periods of time, while maintaining a control mechanism in the phonological store. The visuo-spatial sketch pad processes and stores visual and spatial information. (Towse, 1998; Baddeley, 1986).

Starting in the 1980s, investigators have attempted to measure the effectiveness of working memory during information processing. Their work has approached this task through attempts to measure working memory efficiency, working memory capacity, and working memory effectiveness (Daneman & Tardif, 1987; Shah & Miyake, 1996).

In essence, every step in the Atkinson and Shiffrin process is designated as some level of memory. In this chapter, the focus is on long-term memory, sometimes referred to as long-term store (Atkinson and Shiffrin 1968), and most recently working memory has been under review as a part of short-term store (Baddeley 1998).

Atkinson and Shiffrin considered memory to have three major constituents. The long term memory system was concerned with storing information over extensive periods of time and was fed by a short term memory that acted as a controller, feeding in new information and selecting particular processes for pulling information out of the long term memory. The short term system was itself fed by a series of sensory registers which were essentially micro memories associated with perception. These registers acted as a system for selecting and collating sensory information, and could be viewed as an essential component of perception. (Baddeley 1999)

It is remarkable that critical studies of memory have continued to flourish for more than 100 years. William James, in 1890, often associated with the *functionalist school* of psychology, was among the first scholars to scientifically study memory. He later expanded his work to include selective memory and attention (1890).

Over the past forty years, studies of memory and some of its selected components (attention, perception, etc.) have emerged from different experimental initiatives that have been reported theoretically, empirically, and from sensory-neural perspectives. These areas of memory research have been initiated in various fields including, but not limited to, cognitive psychology, experimental psychology, neuroscience, pharmacology, physiology, biology, human development, child development, and artificial intelligence (Squire and Butters 1984).

What has been lacking in all of this fury is any serious effort to create a compatible context for studies within disciplines, which would enable a scientific concentration on important theoretical traditions to emerge (Tulving 2002). In this context, as of this writing, too little serious attention has been given to studies of memory and cognitive processing by educators.

The past thirty years of memory scholarship have witnessed a trend away from structural theories dealing with memory storage and their capacity in cognitive processing toward a neural emphasis.

It is also true that behavioral approaches to studies of memory and behavior dominated the field of psychology from the 1920s through the 1960s. This was during a period when behavioral psychology was at its peak and it was common practice to use animals in studies, the results of which were generalized to human behavior.

There remain, however, classroom practices that were originally developed from behaviorist theories. Some practices never left education, while others have been reintroduced. The most compelling approach still remaining is the requirement that teachers state objectives for lessons in behavioral terms. It is acceptable to state that "Children will recite from memory the Pythagorean theorem"; an objective that states "Children will learn the Pythagorean theorem" is not acceptable. Objectives must be stated as observable behaviors.

Emphasis on cognitive processing in psychology has paralleled similar interests of linking cognitive psychology with studies of memory. In cognitive neuroscience, memory is theorized as the final stage in the cognitive process known as learning.

In psychology, learning is deemed to have occurred when information is stored in long-term memory. In education, learning must be confirmed by information that is retrieved from long-term memory. This has given rise to an enormously large testing movement in teaching and learning. Steps in the learning process being cited in this book are experience, attention, perception, knowledge acquisition, memory, and retrieval—in that order.

Despite lingering interests in behaviorist principles, some work done during this early period remains respected in today's scientific community. A significant theory of memory and information-processing literature was published in the late 1960s and is considered a classic by some

(Atkinson and Shiffrin 1968). Referred to as the *store model,* Atkinson and Shiffrin trace sensory input into three flexibly defined stages, starting with sensory store (attention), then to short-term store, and ending with long-term store. Missing here are the experiences that occur during human consciousness, and the perception that captures our attention in order for sensory stimulation to start.

There have been many variations on the store model, some suggesting that there is little or no difference between short- and long-term store and that the two areas should be folded into one (Melton 1963). There have also been shifts in the study of memory that have served to emphasize aspects of the theory less related to the storage capacity than to the total accumulation of information and retrieval.

Others have suggested that greater attention should have been given to the *transfer* (movement from one store to another) of information as well as the storage of information. And still others have suggested that inattention to distinctive differences in perceptual modes poses serious flaws at the level of sensory store.

Students and scholars involved in intellectual discussions concerning memory and its various capacities for storage should bear in mind that graphic descriptions of sensory, short-term, and long-term stores are intended for perceptual understanding. The boxes depicting graphic descriptions are metaphors and not "boxes in the head."

On the other hand, graphic descriptions depicting the state and functions of neurons, dendrites, axons, and the cell body (in other chapters) are attempts at actual replications.

SENSATIONS AND TYPES OF EXPERIENCE

A major criticism of the Atkinson and Shiffrin model came from Engelkamp and Zimmer, who identified an inattention to significant variations in modes of human experiences (1994).

For example, studies have reported that writing improves memory traces for pictures but not for words (Durso and Johnson 1980). Nelson, Metzler, and Reed (1974) have suggested that memory for pictures is more lasting than verbal descriptions of the same pictures.

In these examples, words that are written and words that are spoken are still words, but the experiences that bring these words to the attention of the perceiver might differ.

Other questions still remain about the state of sensory information derived from an experience to which the individual attends in different modes. For example, does memory for a landscape last longer if the sensory register transmits a landscape view on a large television screen or a view of the same image as presented in painted watercolor? Or does a view displayed from a photographic slide, while at the same time the perceiver is listening to a recorded description of the same scene, improve memory?

And how would each of these experiences influence memory when compared to an in-person experience similar to that of the photographer? The store model does not report how variability in modalities might affect memory power and ultimately modify interpretations by the experience.

A response to some of these concerns can be found in Atkinson and Shiffrin (1968).

> The character of information in short term store does not depend necessarily upon the form of the sensory input. For example, a word presented visually may be encoded from the visual sensory register into an auditory short-term store. Since the auditory short-term system will play a major role in subsequent discussions, we shall use the abbreviation a-v-l to stand for auditory-verbal-linguistic store. The triple term is used because, as we shall see, it is not easy to separate these three functions. (92)

Studies have suggested a central control system that acts to partially distribute attention, as well as identify different types of attention (Shallice 1974, 1988). This approach replaces *short-term memory* with *working memory* and a *central executive* component for supervising attention (Baddeley 1986).

Despite these criticisms, however, the 1960s work of Atkinson and Shiffrin remains a commonly supported theoretical framework in the study of cognition and memory in university classrooms today. It also retains a significant place in educational psychology and educational methods in textbooks.

MEMORY, PERFORMANCE, AND
KNOWLEDGE ACQUISITION

When teachers think about memory, it often involves the student's proactive process of memorizing a poem or a speaking part in a school dramatic production. Obviously, these are important school experiences from which students can derive useful knowledge, but it is a rather limited view of the role of memory in our lives.

Psychologists have been reporting for the past thirty years how memory power might vary by type of perceptual experience. For example, a teacher might be concerned about conditions under which Michael can demonstrate having memorized his part in the school play and avoid embarrassingly forgetful episodes when moving about the stage in front of a real audience. Is it possible that a solution to Michael's memory limitations for this particular content might be found in an inquiry concerning variability in memory power when motor manipulation is involved?

Superior memory is consistently reported when the *act of doing* is compared to *thinking about doing*. When a group of children was instructed to *draw* simple meaningful objects, their memory was greater when compared to the act of *imagining and seeing* the objects (Paivio and Csapo 1973). In a similar study, Perrig and Hofer (1989) reported superior recall and recognition after *tracing* outlines of two-digit numbers, when compared to children only *imagining* tracing the numbers.

In several other important studies, comparisons have been made between picture/concept memory enhancements and word/concept memory enhancements. It has been reported consistently that concepts associated with words are forgotten more quickly than concepts associated with pictures (Nelson, Metzler, and Reed 1974; Pellegrino, Siegel, and Dhawan 1976).

Within the past few years, a series of events has created a considerable amount of study on long-term working memory (Gobet 2000a). Ericsson and Kintsch (1995) introduced the most well-known model. They explained that experts, unlike the rest of us, store information in long-term memory through a rapid process utilizing two mechanisms: the use of long-term working memory through structures developed for retrieval and the other involving an elaboration of long-term memory patterns.

Gobet (2000b) rejected the idea of long-term working memory, detailing alternative means through which chess experts continue to retain and demonstrate their performance skill. The explanation of long-term working memory, according to Gobet, involved integrated memory structures housed in original long-term memory, as previously defined.

RETENTION AND MEMORY

The word *retention* is often used in conjunction with memory. This book devotes a chapter to retrieval, which is also often used in conjunction with retention.

For example, Carla, a sixth grader, arises in the early morning, washes her face, brushes her teeth, and gets dressed. After preparing and eating morning cereal, she walks to the end of the street on which she lives to wait for the school bus. Carla has been going through this early morning ritual for four months. After arriving at school, in the absence of an unusual encounter, Carla seldom remembers being picked up by the bus, where the bus stops on the way to school, or the arrival of the bus at her school.

Most of us, like Carla, seldom remember our morning rituals or at which traffic lights we stopped on the way to work. The same is true when we leave our workplace for home. Why does this happen? Experiences along our journey have laid down traces, and more than likely some registered in our memory. In the absence of a special incident to interrupt our mundane ritual, traces will probably decay.

For educators, retrieval is assumed when students achieve positive tests scores derived from paper-and-pencil performances. Teachers usually accept tests and similar indicators as reliable reports that information has been retained.

Some education systems go so far as to designate in advance a score that must be attained by students as proof that a predetermined minimum amount of information has been retained to avoid repeating a grade, or failing to graduate. Parent advocacy groups have labeled this practice *high-stakes testing.*

The use of retention in this context makes it synonymous with learning. Deese and Hulse (1967) reported that it is expected that individuals will naturally forget some of what has been stored. Even information remaining in memory cannot be retrieved completely. Deese and Hulse designed an equation that depicted retention as what remains after what was forgotten is subtracted from the amount recalled (1967).

CHILDHOOD MEMORY

Memory described by Piaget in his concrete operations stage (knowledge of the world) is called *semantic memory.* Semantic memory includes labels and associated meanings, names, and words used in describing acts and how things work. For the child to retrieve large amounts of nonverbal information at the right time, there needs to be shared experiences between the learner and someone older who is more knowledgeable about the world than the recipient.

The participation in an experience with a more knowledgeable person is basic to theories of Piaget and Vygotsky. Vygotsky is very explicit about children adding information to their memory through interactions with older persons (Vygotsky 1930). Piaget is less explicit, suggesting that thoughts stored in the child's memory are influenced by the child's level of development (maturation) (Ginsburg and Opper 1969). Educators refer to Piaget's level of development as *readiness.*

By the age of twelve, children have memorized extraordinarily large vocabularies. They know the names of all of the major players in their favorite sport, television characters, parts and functions of machines (such as automobiles and computers), the names of streets, towns, stores, and practically all of the words that describe color, taste, shape, size, and odor of foods, plants, animals, and much more.

In the 1980s, a popular theme called *cultural literacy* recommended to parents and educators that basic teaching and learning problems in education could be corrected through the memorization of selected essential facts (Kett, Trefil, and Hirsch 1987). It was not surprising that the list of facts suggested for memorization was liberally sprinkled with patriotism, citizenship, and civics. Today, the direct instruction approach is commonly practiced.

Sometimes referred to as the *transfer model,* "direct instruction" suggests that educators at various levels of the hierarchy determine what students should know and then transfer this information to the teacher. The teacher transfers this information to students by telling. In turn, the student learns from memorizing what he or she is told by the teacher. The circle is complete when "what students should know" is built into the test (Feinberg 1998).

The essential fact recommended in the *curriculum for cultural literacy* is largely memorizing unimaginative details, such as the location of major cities, state capitals, facts about U.S. presidents, and major events in history (Hirsch 1993). More recently, Hirsch has been more muted about students memorizing content and the promotion of national uniformity in school curriculum.

This appeared to many educators to be a waste of memory for children to walk around with this set of facts at hand, one that is easily accessible in the nearest library or on the Internet.

During childhood experiences in their towns and cities, major sports teams will capture the attention of children, especially during final play-off games. During the championship encounters, many children who are not particularly successful in school mathematics or reading assignments appear to have little difficulty figuring out the meaning of batting averages and remembering them. They also remember how to spell the names of their favorite athletes.

It is also true that many children who do not read well in school have little trouble memorizing the words of songs that have captured the attention of their friendship group. This works for many students because they wish to memorize particular things that they consider important, relevant to their experience, and things in which they wish to engage.

Educators strive to increase the learner's semantic memory by influencing the child's thinking about new meanings—to enable the acquisition of new knowledge by blending incoming knowledge with concepts presently existing in long-term memory.

VISUAL MEMORY

Is a concept of visual memory valid? If yes, how about separating auditory, olfactory, and tactile memories? Should memory be discussed in this segmented manner rather than conceptualizing all sensory inputs into a single long-term memory?

Sensory memory is basic to Gestalt psychology. Gestaltism in this book is described in chapter 3 on perception, and was viewed by Piaget as a complete intellectual model, though he rejected the theory of Gestaltism (Piaget 1969).

In considering stage plays and motion picture experiences, visual memory is an essential tool for artists and technicians. Consider the stage play with performers entering and departing the dramatic experience. Sometimes the audience is asked to consider that upon leaving the stage, a particular character is going somewhere when she leaves the stage while the performance remains in view.

The character leaving the stage announces that she plans to go home. Within a relatively short period of time the audience is expected to have remembered the actress' earlier lines, and visualize from memory her presence in her off-stage home. Being an important part of the plot, the playwright depends upon the visual memory of the audience to put together the performer's having left the stage, while it remains fixed on the present scene.

It was a major task for Laurie Dickson in 1890, before "moving pictures," to conceptualize the making of the world's first motion picture. Dickson filmed his assistant with his newly developed "kinetoscope" in a motion picture titled *Monkey Shines*, which lasted about five seconds. The act of the naming of a motion picture with a title similar to its story line was done to ensure that audiences and historians would remember this achievement and its inventor. Some time later, Dickson and Ott teamed with Thomas Alva Edison, who constructed a studio in 1893.

For the first time, viewers had to attend to moving images in an enclosed space, which had continuity from the past to the immediate present, and a continually evolving future. These three phases could also be repeated. Working sensory memory enabled the viewer to experience a continuous story, using sensory register, short-term memory, long-term memory, and working memory to place a moving picture event in a continuous context (Schwarz 2003).

The Great Train Robbery, the first complete one-reel story, was shown to audiences in their first experience in viewing life-sized pictures in motion and continuity, without language, from beginning to end. In a darkened viewing room, Edison had to rely on the sensory memory of his audience to piece together a story from memory. Viewers first invoked their attention because their curiosity brought them to the experience.

The audience then committed their short-term memory to events of the immediacy; doing so enabled them to pair their short-term memory with continually unfolding events. Several stages of memory were called upon to follow the flow of the story. Finally, the audience recalled the filmed story's past, reflected on the present, and anticipated the end.

Audiences frame a future from their own reflection; probably a retelling took place among family and friends who had heard about this futuristic experience.

In France in 1895, photographic inventors Auguste and Louis Lumière patented a projector. They rented a basement cafe designed to seat 100 people, but only thirty-three attended. The brothers were the first to show a "news reel." Scenes included in the short film were the feeding of a baby and an approaching train that caused the audience to flee from the cafe in fear of being crushed (Schwarz 2003).

So, if you are still asking, "What is memory?" and a surgeon were seeking to find it, how would she locate it? Larry Squire (1987) has articulated some revealing clues.

> Memory is both distributed and localized. Memory is distributed in that no single memory center exists, and many parts of the nervous system participate in the representation of a single event. Memory is localized in that the representation of a single event involves a limited number of brain systems and pathways, and each part of the brain contributes differently to the representation. The brain is a highly differentiated and specialized organ. Those areas of the brain within which memory is equivalently represented probably contain no more than a thousand neurons. Each of these "equivalent sets" of neurons must represent only a narrow "microfeature" of information. In the case of visual object memory, perhaps in the case of memory for any complex event, the neocortex is a likely storehouse of representations. (123)

Currently, theoretical approaches concerning working memory are providing various models. Short-term memory theory originally suggested the holding of chunks of information for a period of time for almost immediate use. From the original work of Atkinson and Shiffrin (1968), short-term memory was paired with working memory in that it was available for early use. Baddeley (1986) paired working memory with attention, now known as *short-term working memory.*

MEMORY AS METAPHOR

On September 11, 2001, residents in the city of New York experienced a tragedy. An attack on the New York World Trade Center's twin towers resulted in the complete destruction of several buildings along with the deaths of thousands of occupants.

To ensure a *remembrance* of the victims, events of mourning were scheduled at the site of the tragedy and in various parts of the city. These events, in part, were held to relieve some of the pain of *emotional memories* of experiences by relatives of the victims, and also to revere the dead and enable others in the city to satisfy some of their emotional memories.

Here, emotional memory of those killed in the collapse of the towers becomes embedded in the memory of all U.S. citizens living at the time of the incident. The retelling of that tragedy for those born after the event establishes a common history. During the aftermath, it was reported that approximately 3,000 occupants in the building were killed. This tragedy ultimately became a remembrance for the world.

In 1989, approximately the same number of civilians were killed by the U.S. invasion of Panama when 26,000 U.S. troops attacked the country to search for one man—Manuel Noriega. After the attack, thousands of mostly impoverished Panamanian victims of the invasion were buried in mass graves by the U.S. military, following egregious military acts. The United Nations voted to sanction this military action of the United States in Panama, but most U.S. media ignored that vote.

These horrific atrocities remain in the emotional memories of Panamanian citizens, as well as in the memories of their family members who were interned in U.S. concentration camps set up in Panama. This invasion will be shared among Panamanian residents and families, and will become their permanent remembrance. The emotional memory of the Panama tragedy will affect far fewer people than those with emotional memories of the World Trade Center because much of the Panamanian tragedy fell prey to poor media coverage in the United States. The United States, sometimes with force, restricted world media coverage of the invasion, but it is also true that U.S. media demonstrated very little interest in disseminating information about the atrocities that followed (Ryan 1993).

Avishai Margalit (2002) calls this type of memory *memory of emotions*. He would also call both tragedies episodic memories. As traces of memory, Margalit suggests that they would be equally important as remembrances of emotions.

In his recent book *The Ethics of Memory*, Margalit focuses on semantic and episodic memory. In his view, past memories can be either episodic or semantic; for ethical issues, his chosen paradigm encompasses memory of past emotions. In perceiving ethics of memory as a metaphor, Margalit identifies a danger in memories of past emotions.

In this regard, hatred inherited by today's generations from remembrances of stories told to us by our ancestors runs the risk of poisoning our relationship with innocent descendants of the original perpetrators of atrocities (Margalit 2002).

This concept, as applied to the events in the emotional memories of citizens in the United States and Panama, informs that, as years pass, citizens in neither geographic domain should retrieve emotional memories captured by hate for present populations because of acts perpetrated by their ancestors.

In pursuing Margalit's thesis, neither Panamanians nor Jews should harbor emotions based on the acts of previous U.S. or German generations; neither should Native Americans or blacks retain negative attitudes toward white U.S. citizens of today for earlier genocide (Native Americans) or slavery (blacks) (Bernal 1987). To undergird his thesis, Margalit points out that neither today's Germans nor U.S. whites participated in atrocities of the past.

There are substantial reasons for suggesting that citizens of the United States not retain negative attitudes toward perpetrators of acts of terrorism in our history. When such acts become historical memories, hatreds should be laid to rest. And we should expect victims of our acts of terrorism to respond in kind.

Others have pointed out that the United States, though justified in its anger, should remember that its own foreign policy, over the years, has perpetrated similar acts on other countries.

Citizens in the United States probably remember the frequency of our country's invasions of other countries. Citizens in those countries on the receiving end also remember their loss of property and life. The U.S. invasion of Vietnam occurred in 1965, followed by the illegal bombing of Cambodia from 1970 to 1973. The invasion of Grenada occurred in 1983, followed by the bombing in Panama in 1989. And, despite the fact that the president has declared victory, in 2003, the U.S. invasion and the occupation of Iraq continues along with the deaths of U.S. soldiers and Iraqi civilians.

The U.S. campaign against international terrorism is a reasonable response to the attacks on the twin towers and loss of life in New York City, Washington, D.C., and Pennsylvania. This campaign, however, is being enacted in an atmosphere of memories of similar U.S. acts against citizens in other countries. Noam Chomsky articulates this theme with depth and clarity in his book *9/11*.

The concept of learning begs for more attention and study on retrieval. The value of retrieval in today's classroom cannot be overestimated. With greater attention being focused on student performance, school systems are experiencing media attention focused on the narrowly constructed and overvalued performance scores of their students. Moreover, some districts are associating student performance with evaluations of teacher competence. These policies invest high stakes in narrowly defined skill teaching and student test performance.

Six

Retrieval

> No sooner does an approaching hour become the present for us than it sheds all its charms, only to regain them, it is true, on the roads of memory, when we have left that hour behind us, and so long as our soul is vast enough to disclose deep *perspectives.*
>
> —Marcel Proust (emphasis added)

The process of retrieval (occasionally referred to as *remembrance*) and recall (also discussed under the topic of *forgetting*) is often called *learning by heart.* Many common phrases suggest that memory is stored in the heart. This is especially true when certain memories are related to an emotional experience. Phrases like "heartfelt" and "heartwarming" are examples. Some believe that the truth only can be "spoken from the heart." We inherited the belief that memory, intellectual activity, and emotion are located in the heart from early Greek scholars and philosophers.

This is an example of the enormous influence that Western philosophers like Plato, Aristotle, Pythagoras, and Socrates have had upon our thinking. During their time, their ideas were rarely challenged. Socrates, however, never put his ideas in writing but had a group of young learners with whom he walked about the neighborhoods holding discussions that were initiated by him or his students. This method of knowledge building between student and scholar bears the name of Socrates, and has become known as the *Socratic method.* Aristotle is remembered in the academy for what we call *Aristotelian logic*, a form of logic that rests primarily on practical, empirical thought.

These great Western philosophers were occasionally wrong. Aristotle was wrong when he argued that the heart was the center of knowledge and the brain served to cool the blood. Despite such errors, much of their thinking, nonetheless, remains in our belief today. Even in error, Western philosophy continues to influence our thought, and it is common to suggest that, emotionally, humans experiencing tragedy can have a "broken heart" or in a state of worry or disappointment have a "heavy heart."

The influence of Western philosophers extends to the scholarly community as well. In the 1978 edition of the *Oxford Dictionary of Quotations*, one can find a reference to *learning by heart*: "learning poetry (and even prose) by heart for repetition" (iii). It is assumed here that learning by heart ensures permanent knowledge and guarantees retrieval.

D. E. Broadbent (1958), a member of the applied psychology unit of the Medical Research Council in Cambridge, England, extended this error in the scholarly community when he wrote "Anyone familiar with modern learning theory is aware that a list of items *learnt by heart* are not equally difficult throughout" (emphasis added, 217).

In reality, one cannot learn in this manner because the heart has no cognitive capacity!

Pythagoras (circa 580–500 B.C.E.), a Greek philosopher, was correct when he gave us the *Pythagorean theorem*, which has been memorized by most of us who have taken eighth-grade geometry: the square of the hypotenuse of a right triangle is equal to the sum of squares of the other two sides. This discovery by Pythagoras has remained in our schools for more than 2,000 years! Pythagoras and his followers were interested in the relationship between humans and the environment, and studied these phenomena through mysticism, mathematics, and religion. Pythagoras was also among the first to recognize the role of the brain in memory and learning.

Information that has entered long-term memory is information that has been learned. Learning is a sensory-neural process that transfers information from experience and perception to short-term memory and finally to long-term memory.

By now, from reading this text, you are aware that current theories about learning suggest that working memory is currently affiliated with short term storage. Information can also decay (disappear) at any point along this pathway, or it can successfully reach long-term memory and become integrated with previously implanted long-term memory traces and become *knowledge*. Neuroscience and psychology reference this process as cognition. Retrieval of information is now being studied as a system of short-term memory activation, a system that enables an ongoing access to information (Nairne 2002).

Following the gradual reduction of the concentration of psychological studies on behaviorism, a major concentration in cognitive studies emerged on working memory (Atkinson and Shiffrin 1968; Squire 1984; Nairne 2002). It is that area of cognitive processing that enables the retrieval of a modest quantity of ten digits (similar to a phone number, for example) at almost any given time (Baddeley 1986). Working memory is that knowledge to which we have almost immediate access. Our capacity to know and understand is truly a working capacity enabling and directing our daily lives more often than we are aware. Some have even referred to this capacity as *short-term working memory* (Nairne 2002).

For example, working memory is working as we follow the steps required in getting dressed, making coffee, reading this book, starting our car, driving to our destination, and making simple mental math computations when a purchase is made at the coffee shop. *Working memory* is an appropriate label because it is frequently "put to work" by the organism (Klatzky 1984; Baddeley 1999).

We expect that in the absence of specific attention, working memory will automatically be available for our use. When it is in use, however, it occasionally calls for attention. Most of the time this will be true and it will, upon command, enable humans to access knowledge acquired from hundreds of daily experiences. Our access to memory is called *retrieval* because we are able to retrieve information that is stored in memory.

During our schooling experiences, we have all used a mnemonic system to retrieve information for a test or to memorize a phrase or poem. During this process, we used learned information that is related in some way to the information to be retrieved. This previously known information could be a, b, c, d, for example. We then lay down a memory trace that associate these letters with the information to be retrieved. We selected a, b, c, d because the information to be remembered is related in some manner to these letters. When retrieval is called for, it should be simpler to retrieve a, b, c, d and that will enable us to recall the more complex information that we have associated with a, b, c, d.

> It is often claimed that memory resembles a vast library, an analogy that has its limitations, but which can be very useful. One way in which memory and a library are closely similar is in the extent to which both will only work efficiently if information is stored in a structured systematic way, with retrieval of information depending on this initial cataloging or encoding. (Baddeley 1990, 191)

Under certain unusual and infrequent conditions, this access will not be available. One of these unusual circumstances is called the *tip-of-the-tongue (TOT) phenomenon* and is covered later in this chapter.

It has also been reported recently that short-term memory and working memory should not be considered synonymous (Nairne 2002). It is pointed out that information in a form that makes it immediately accessible can also be considered a mnemonic entity, but the process of retrieval actually starts with an activation of long-term memory (permanent knowledge). Further, retrieval is enabled through "online" processing by establishing a memory trace in short-term memory.

The retrievability of information stored in long-term memory has been of interest to the research community for some time now. The idea that some individuals might have limited access to their knowledge that has been stored for a length of time has also been studied (Shiffrin and Schneider 1977; Squire 1984). Recent studies have examined *long-term potentiation* (LTP) as an approach to placing basic neurological principles into the understanding of patterns of learning (Baddeley 1999).

There has also been interest in developmental studies of the integration of learning principles and memory. That interest has emerged from studies with infants and toddlers. Rose, Feldman, and Jankowski (2001), for example, studied *recognition memory* among infants. Greater visual attention and recognition memory were reported for full-term infants when they were compared to their preterm counterparts.

Two experimental modes were designed to investigate memory retrieval for musical experiences among infants. Infants were exposed to two different passages of Mozart movements daily for two weeks. They reported that infants retained familiarized music and the experience influenced listening preferences. Listening preferences were measured by removing familiar passages from the total music experience (Saffran, Griepentrog, and Gregory 2001).

Blischak and McDaniel (1995), from a study of normally developing kindergarten children with communication disorders, reported that children demonstrated superior memory performance for word and word-enhanced conditions when compared to experiences involving the pairing of small or large drawings with written words. Subjects were encouraged to use alternative patterns of communicating preferences.

Robinson (1995) matched memory, attention, and noticing to determine if a relationship existed between the three variables during the acquisition of a second language. Robinson reported that variations in memory retrieval were related to processing demands and noticing by the subject.

Conceptually, experiences that capture our attention have entered the first step of encoding. Encoded information ultimately becomes stored in long-term memory and thus retrieved for use (Klatzky 1984).

REFLECTION AND MEMORIES

It is not uncommon for teachers and students, in their respective discussion groups, to become reflective about events of the school day or at year's end. Teachers are also reflective in the presence of peers and comparable professionals. These reflections are conversations about memories.

Reflecting on the past and relating events and experiences to the present and future can also be a family activity, where older members of different ages share their memories and younger members listen to the memories of others. Vygotskian theory of child development is based upon these events (Vygotsky 1934).

People commonly share memories that involve retrieving knowledge from previous experiences, and in an existential manner, repeat and re-experience (in a more current context) selected earlier experiences through the process of retrieval. This oral tradition has occurred in family and friends groups from the beginning of human existence. It is an oral experience through which we are connected to our past, and it provides a vision for the future.

RETRIEVAL OF A FAMILY EXPERIENCE

James Baldwin (1924–1987), an African American essayist, wrote a letter to his nephew as a means of sharing with the general public the reflections of the experience of growing up black in the United States. Baldwin's use of a "Letter to My Nephew" was an existential metaphor for his own experience.

In describing interactions between self, his father, his brother, and now his young nephew in the context of society, Baldwin chose the celebration of the 100th anniversary of the *Emancipation Proclamation.*

"Letter to My Nephew" was published in Baldwin's nonfiction work *The Fire Next Time.* Among other things, reflections on his memories of the men in their family were described to his nephew.

> Dear James:
>
> I have begun this letter five times and torn it up five times. I keep seeing your face, which is also the face of your father and my brother. Like him you are tough, dark, vulnerable, moody—with a very definite tendency to sound truculent because you want no one to think you are soft. You may be like your grandfather in this, I don't know, but certainly both of you, you and your father, resemble him very much physically. Well, he is dead, he never saw you, and he had a terrible life; he was defeated long before he died, because at the bottom of his heart, he really believed what white people said about him. This is one of the reasons that he became so holy. . . . I have known both of you all of your lives, have carried your daddy in my arms and on my shoulders, kissed and spanked him and watched him learn to walk. (Baldwin 1963, 3)

EPISODIC AND SEMANTIC MEMORY

Knowledge gained from experiences in general is called *semantic* memory. This knowledge remains long after we have forgotten the experiences from which we acquired the information.

Episodic memory is the name used for knowledge gained from experiences that can be termed episodes. Studies of episodic memory have been in neurological and cognitive processing literature for some time now (Tulving 1972).

> Episodic memory refers to memory for past events in an individual's life. This system represents information concerning temporarily dated episodes that can be later recollected. Episodic memory stores the cumulated events of one's life, an individual's autobiography. Semantic memory refers to knowledge of the world. This system represents organized information such as facts, concepts, and vocabulary. The content of semantic memory is explicitly known and available for recall. Unlike episodic memory, however, semantic memory has no necessary temporal landmarks. It does not refer to particular events in a person's past. (Squire 1984)

Schools, classrooms, and their accommodating play and social areas are replete with experiences that are processed as semantic and episodic memory. Children and their teachers participate in academic events and recreational activities that create individual and group encounters. As events and experiences unfold in classrooms and play areas, teachers are frequently called upon to resolve conflicts. Conflict resolution often rests on memories of participating children and on children who are observers. In resolving conflicts, teachers must allow each asked child ample time to recall an episode. In the process of seeking a resolution, the teacher must not reject a child's interpretation of events as recalled from their memory (see phenomenology and existentialism in chapter 3).

As children describe their memory of an episode, the role of the teacher is to encourage the group to agree on a resolution while not appearing to take sides (Kostelnik et al. 1998).

Buckner and Barch (1999) in their study of episodic memory reported that a network of brain areas were active during events that could be classified as episodic. Selected areas of the brain were color coded to enable the more active regions to display a bright red color. The display revealed that the right anterior frontal region is more selectively activated by episodic retrieval tasks.

> An important function of the human brain is learning and memory. Environmental demands on memory vary greatly. In some instances, we are

required to keep information "online" for active use for several seconds, whereas in other instances, we are required to store information for retrieval days, weeks, or even years later. Take, for example, the long-term memory of unique events, commonly called episodic memory. This form of memory is characterized by having a unique context associated with a learning episode. Episodic memory can be seen as a specialized form of more general memory functions that permits the storage and retrieval of facts and bits of information. However, episodic memory differs in that it requires access to the context and personal participation in an event that mark it as a specific episode in memory. A set of interdependent brain regions is clearly critical to the successful learning, storage, and retrieval of episodic memories. (Buckner and Barch 1999, 1)

Retrieval has been reported to prevail along a continuum from passive to active availability. Active processing (sometimes called *controlled processing*) requires a considerable capacity to remain operative and is therefore limited. On the other hand, *passive processing* (sometimes called *automatic processing*) can be operative with fewer demands on the cognitive system. Active processing includes decisions, strategies, and retrieval from long-term memory (see the example of the basketball game in chapter 4). Passive processing involves encoding of spatial information (Hasher and Zacks 1979).

As people go about their lives, unpleasant things can happen through injury or infection. Through aging, people commonly experience limited retrieval capacity. Here, studies have reported a connection between high-order processing and the aforementioned active processing (Fuld 1976). Methods employed to determine the extent to which a failure to recall impairs active retrieval, or the overall capacity to retrieve, utilize divided-attention tasks (McDowall 1981).

People who experience amnesia do not have memory that works. Amnesiacs are unable to reflect on prior information stored in long-term memory. We now know, from a study by Squires (1982), that amnesiacs can learn new information that has been acquired through perceptual motor skills and recently placed in their long-term memory.

Structural information theory (Atkinson and Shiffrin 1968) and the enveloping sensory-neural system (senses and our central nervous system), along with how they are involved in information tracking, are covered in chapter 1.

From thinking to direct behavior, the individual controls the use of the retrieval system. The availability of retrievable information for use by the individual is a neural function associated with cognitive processing. A system of executive directing has been theorized as the processing of knowledge for human use. Starting in the 1970s, scholars have identified several systems for the retrieval process. Among them are the *central executive* function by Norris and Jones (1990) and Towse (1998), the *control for information processing (CIP)* by Norman and Shallice (1986), and the *supervisory attentional system (SAS).* Each of these functions or systems has been proposed as a model of the central executive in working memory. These labels commonly refer to the intentional act of activating one's body of knowledge, for which retrieval is an essential element.

MEMORY RETRIEVAL

Retrieval as a Measure of Performance

In the present-day language of educators and psychometricians, it is common to employ instruments (tests) designed to measure performance, and to label the paper-and-pencil results deriving from such measures as *learning.* This approach does not, however, determine the full extent to which learning has taken place, nor the type of information learned.

The intellectual capacity of an individual can be quantified in various ways. The measurement of cognitive abilities in children remains more an art than a science. Given the state of the art, investigations of the instrument are more reasonable than using the present-day instruments to test the individual. Alan Kaufman (1992) suggests "Any intelligence test for . . . assessment requires the examiner to go beyond the simple IQ and try to make sense out of why the child scored the way he or she did. And proper use of IQ tests with the gifted or the potentially gifted children demands that they be used in conjunction with other tests and criteria" (158).

Various tests now employed by educators at all levels attempt to measure what individual students, or students as a group (class, school, city, state, country, etc.), have "learned." For placement in gifted-type classes, and classes for the academically challenged, tests are mandatory.

Local public media consistently compare the performance scores of students by city, county, state, and country. For each student, a number is reported to enable the general public to make a simple comparison between children in their school, city, or country, with others. In the political atmosphere of such reporting, it is generally accepted that these scores are true measures of student knowledge. With sunshine laws in most states, group and school scores are available to media and individuals who petition for such information.

It is not surprising that high scores are reported for private and neighborhood schools attended by students from high-income families, and lower scores reported for schools attended mostly by children from lower-income families. Children in families where their parents are employed to construct the tests (or others employed at that level) are exposed to a different dinner-table conversation than children from families whose parents are employed as laborers. A student's experience can be a narrowing or expanding factor and there is considerable work in the academic community to increase the amount, while narrowing the type of information considered essential (Kett, Trefil, and Hirsch 1987).

Students with differing types of family experiences might acquire significant amounts of knowledge from their experiences, but tests do not give equal weight to all knowledge. And some knowledge, referred to as "street smarts," comes from experiences that are not available in classrooms, especially to children in higher-income communities.

Scholars have reported that testing has many serious limitations (Kamin 1974; Kaufman 1992). Among black learners, for example, their achievement test scores are expected to fluctuate over time. It has been reported that they tend to gain then lose ground as support for education raises and falls (Kamin 1996). Neither psychologists nor educators know the extent to which performance on tests matches individual capacity of working memory.

The Measurement of Retrieval Capacity

Over various intervals of time, classroom teachers present segments of information that they expect children to "learn." Educators attempt to access the learner's retention capacity by administering to groups of children a paper-and-pencil test. Various tests are designed to measure achievement in such subject areas as mathematics, reading, science, and social studies, for example. It has also been pointed out that IQ tests are in reality achievement tests.

Intelligence tests purport to measure general intelligence by tapping into knowledge that can be retrieved from long-term memory. Performances on IQ tests correlate significantly with scores derived from achievement tests. Tests are designed to measure performance; school performance is highly valued.

Performance scores are usually reported by schools in local and national media. It is not surprising that for various reasons, critics attempt to measure performance, and label it something related to a desirable human trait. IQ became a likely candidate.

The idea of an intelligence test to measure the retrieval of information for academic performance can be traced to Simon and Binet who, in the early 1900s, were contracted by the Paris minister of public instruction to devise a test to identify children suspected of being mentally challenged so that they could be properly placed for special attention.

Alfred Binet (1857–1911), a French psychologist, unimpressed with formal studies that led to a degree in law, started to study psychology by reading books on his own. During this period, he discovered the writings of John Stuart Mill, who at the time was considered an *associationist*. Associationism was a category of reductionist psychology; its adherents believed that association and reassociation of perceptions could explain consciousness. Mill held that intelligence could be explained by the laws of associationist theory.

Binet, after identifying with the associationists for a period of time, started to develop a view from his reading of psychology that differed significantly from Mill. From his reading, Binet nurtured a long-time interest in psychology from a neurological perspective.

After receiving an appointment in the neurological laboratory at the Salpêtriére Hospital in Paris, Binet started working with Jean-Martin Charcot, who was intrigued with studies of hypnotism at the time. Binet's interest was so captured by studies of hypnotism that it led to his publishing several papers on the topic. His articles on hypnotism could not be supported scientifically, and this led to an embarrassing public admission by Binet.

Binet's next appointment was at the Sorbonne Laboratory of Experimental Psychology. Here, he became director in 1894 and, about the same time, he became a member of a group of psychologists interested in the study of intelligence in children. Associations in this membership influenced Binet to observe and record the development of his two daughters, and this family activity is thought to have been a major influence on his persistent interest in human intelligence.

Led by Binet in 1904, a select group from the child psychology membership was appointed to a French government commission on the education of retarded children. Their early diagnostic measures were based upon assessing various factors related to reasoning skills, and it was assumed that these selected intellectual abilities (factors) contributed to a single general intelligence.

Specifically, the Binet-Simon scale consisted of thirty performances gradually increasing in difficulty. The first required a performance that was assumed to be of little difficulty for children at any developmental level, even the retarded. The simplest task required a handshake with the examiner. This might be followed by a request that the child repeat three digits, and asked to point to and identify selected body parts. Starting at age two, tasks were developmentally progressed to age six (Fancher 1985).

Binet and Simon defined intelligence more in terms of human adaptation to circumstances and judgment (Piaget) in everyday life than our present-day application.

> Intelligence is a fundamental faculty, the alteration or lack of which, is of the utmost importance for practical life. This faculty is judgment, otherwise called sense, practical sense, initiative, the faculty of adapting one's self to circumstances. A person can be a moron or imbecile if he is lacking in judgment; but with good judgment he can never be either. Indeed the rest of intellectual faculties seem of little importance in comparison with judgment. (Binet and Simon 1916, 42–43)

No single element in defining the measuring of intelligence has survived over time with greater persistence than the theory that intelligence can be determined by this single factor, labeled the *g* factor (Spearman 1904).

The concept of general intelligence as it relates to school performance was introduced in the United States by Stanford University professor Lewis M. Terman in 1916. Terman used the Binet and Simon instrument as a basis for developing the well-known Stanford-Binet test of intelligence. This instrument has undergone various modifications since its introduction and is currently the most widely administered test of intelligence.

As with the Binet and Simon instrument, the Stanford-Binet test of intelligence purports to determine general intelligence from selected factors deemed to be essentials of intellectual performance. The revised Stanford-Binet still provides a single score that purports to reflect general intelligence (Terman and Merrill 1937).

The Wechsler Intelligence Scale for Children-Revised (WISC-R) is the next most commonly used instrument. Both WISC-R and the Stanford-Binet are designed to be administered individually, with the Stanford-Binet emphasizing verbal responses more than the WISC-R. The WISC-R is designed for children six to sixteen, and consists of twelve subtests (two are optional). Half of the items are verbal and half do not require verbal responses (Wechsler 1989).

Almost for the life of the IQ test, various groups have attempted to use the instrument to report differences between and among groups. Ronald Taylor and Stephen Richards (1991) studied the intellectual differences between black, Hispanic, and white children using the WISC-R. Their results reported that black children performed better on verbal tasks, white children scored higher on tasks that required abstract thinking and knowledge of facts, and Hispanic children performed better on visual-spatial tasks. Taylor and Richards cautioned that these results might be indicators of "educational needs" rather than intellectual deficits for any group. Further, they suggested that attention should be given to teaching patterns to accommodate areas of weak performance. These results could also be a proxy for differentiations in cognitive style. Kamin and Isham (1993) have also cast doubt on the reliability of black/white comparisons of performance data using the Spearman hypothesis.

In the 2000s, the state of the art in measuring intelligence among schoolchildren for various purposes, like screening for the placement of children in classes for the gifted, has led to the selection of the Wechsler Intelligence Scale for Children-III (WISC-III), as well as the Wechsler Preschool and Primary Scale of Intelligence-Revised (WPPSI-R). Both tests demonstrate an improvement in acknowledging the subtleties of race and gender. The preschool version has more than 40 percent new items, and the new items in the WISC-III total more than 30 percent. Many experts in the field remain critical of instruments designed to measure the capacity to retrieve knowledge. In order to compensate for an inherent flaw in the most recent version of the WPPSI-R, the test developers added bonus points for speed. In response to this strategy, one reviewer suggested that:

> Giving bonus points for speed to preschool children seems silly from a developmental and common-sense perspective. Sure, brighter children will tend to solve problems more quickly than less intelligent children, and that relationship will hold even at the preschool level. But young children sometimes respond slowly for a variety of reasons that have more to do with maturation or personality. For example, a young child might respond deliberately because of immaturity of experience in test taking, underdeveloped motor coordination, insecurity, or a reflective cognitive style. (Kaufman 1992, 158)

The widespread use of these traditional instruments occurs at a time when information-processing theorists and others are suggesting alternative approaches, and in the process creating a receptive scientific environment for imaginative and inventive constructs. (Montagu, 1999)

Guilford, for example, described intelligence as encompassing five operations (divergent production, convergent production, cognition, memory, and evaluation). The same model included six products (units, classes, relations, systems, implications, and transformation). It also included four content areas (figurative, semantics, behavioral, and symbolic). These three domains would generate 120 cells.

Some cells match abilities typically measured by standardized intelligence tests, whereas others represent a multidimensional structure of intelligence. For example, memory for symbolic relations would subsume operations and a form of content. Guilford conceptualized these measurable abilities as factors that contributed to individual general intelligence.

In his book *Frames of Mind,* Howard Gardner (1983) created a great deal of interest among education practitioners when he proposed that individuals have at least seven different intelligences. Gardner's "intelligences" appeared to be more related to cognitive styles than intelligence; however, the notion that individuals possess more than a single intelligence stimulated a great deal of conversation among practitioners who took their discussions beyond the dominant theory of one-factor intelligence to an idealized version of learning from a subjectively descriptive perspective, rather than from what is known about the original construct accepted as IQ (Morgan 1996).

Spearman (1904) constructed intelligence tests in such a way as to ensure the concept of a single factor, g. In such a design, Spearman started with the idea of a *principal component*, using a single axis, with other abilities projected at right angles and rotated for the highest potential. By selecting a principal component concept and projecting each vector (subordinate factors) onto the axis, Spearman could always yield a single factor—but he conceded that a specific factor might be unique to a particular test. An excellent discussion of this original construct can be found in Stephen Jay Gould's *The Mismeasure of Man* (1981).

A provocative secular humanist, Stephen Jay Gould (1941–2002), made enormous contributions to the public's understanding of science (1977, 1980, 1983). As a professor of zoology at Harvard University, he proposed a theory that became somewhat controversial.

As a supporter of Darwin's ideas, Gould theorized that evolution was not simply a consistently linear process; rather, it progressed intermittently, allowing new species to graduate to life and enter the flow of living things (Gould 2002).

L. L. Thurstone was among the first to suggest that the human organism was far too complex for intellectual activity to be determined solely by a single human factor. In 1938, he developed what he labeled *primary mental abilities* and introduced to the intelligence-testing community multivariate analyses to operationalize his theory. Thurstone's test batteries were developed for three age levels, with approximately six tests designed to measure each separate ability.

Thurstone's theory explained that intelligence cannot be determined by measuring a single ability; rather, multiple factors like verbal ability, deductive reasoning, spatial ability, and perceptual speed are essential to a unified theory of intelligence. Thurstone rejected the principal component approach to factor analysis, and he proposed a rotated factor axis that, in essence, eliminated *g* in the process.

Despite Thurstone's new approach to the reexamination of a seasoned theory, it remained the view of Spearman and his followers that Thurstone's "set of abilities" contained an underlying element common to all measures of ability that could be defined within the framework of *g*. There is some dispute as to the original inventor of factor analysis. Burt claimed this distinction, but most writers give the credit to Spearman. The work of these early theorists still dominates a great deal of today's scholarly thought on the subject of intellectual performance and IQ testing.

Despite the persistence of *g* theorists, the practice of intelligence testing began to incorporate Thurstone's multifactorial analyses. Following Thurstone's publication of a test battery of primary mental abilities, others started to develop multivariate instruments to measure separate abilities.

Gesell (1949), for example, developed an age scale to measure infant development. The Gesell developmental schedules defined five areas of behavior but did not claim these were measures of intelligence. The areas included adaptive behavior (subject's reactions to objects), motor behavior (subject's control of body), language behavior (vocalizations and speech), bodily expression, and personal–social behavior (interpersonal relations). Many of Gesell's followers, however, used the Gesell model to develop instruments to assess these behaviors and labeled their instruments "measures of intelligence."

Almost fifty years later, Howard Gardner (1983) selected Thurstone's primary mental abilities and Gesell's developmental abilities to shape into his theory of seven individual intelligences (Morgan 1996).

At several intervals in the history of various approaches to assessing intelligence, single-factor theorists have had to defend against occasional assaults. It has been suggested that persons have at least seven different intelligences. (Gardner, 1983) The expanded view of what constitutes intelligence has called attention to another construct called *cognitive style.*

Whereas teachers are encouraged to recognize intelligent behavior that might not be tapped by traditional intelligence tests, they must also recognize variations in how learners approach their schoolwork.

It has also been known for some time that personality and temperament are important variables in the teacher–learner relationship. As more attention is being given to the learner, educators become open to the fact that children bring to the learning environment a great deal that needs to be considered in educational planning.

A RETRIEVING PROBLEM

For some time now, studies have reported the phenomenon of having the knowledge that you actually *know* something, but the information cannot be retrieved (Beattie and Coughlan 1999). This has been referred to as the *tip-of-the-tongue phenomenon (TOT)*. Under certain circumstances, the retrieval of knowledge from long-term memory or working memory to a here-and-now experience is not working; causing the TOT interference. Knowing that you know *is* working; trying to retrieve what you know *is not* (Larkin 2000; Widner 1996).

Studies have also reported that when the forgetter is given the first letter of the word to be retrieved, they are better at giving the information with greater achievement than chance success (Brown & McNeill, 1966).

When common knowledge cannot be reported by the knowers, knowers are often able to report items associated with the nonretrievable information along with facts about the individual's unretrieved name (Moses 1988; Wellman 1977). How often might TOT situations occur during an important test, like the SAT? Operating alone, TOT might not pose a frequent problem. However, depending upon the importance of the test, when this possibility is placed with the aforementioned compromises, the negative consequences can be substantial.

Testing situations start with compromises. The first compromise is with the selected items for the test. Here, errors are introduced when the knowledge being tested must be placed in a paper-and-pencil format, and is only representative of what the instrument purports to measure.

This condition is further exacerbated because, in the academy, achievement tests are well supported by a large number of parents and educators who are willing to accept a written response to a question, when the correct written response is actually a substitute for the knowledge being tested. It is also true that learners occasionally have retrievable skills available to them under certain circumstances and not at other times or under testing conditions.

TOT introduces another troublesome variable. Given the tension present in a testing environment, it would not be uncommon for this phenomenon to interfere with the retrieval process. This interference could induce doubt and prevail in a manners so that other known matter is disrupted.

ORAL TRADITIONS

In families and other social groups, it is not uncommon to find at least one person who has poor reading skills. While the Laubach Literacy Program operates worldwide from its headquarters in Syracuse, New York, they claim that there are large numbers of adults with reading skills too inadequate for them to read a third-grade text.

The National Center for Education Statistics does not measure "illiteracy" in the United States. They do, however, measure literacy competence at progressive levels starting with level 1 (one). This level would be unable to read a third-grade text. Of the level 1 readers, 25 to 30 percent are likely to be aged fifty-five to sixty-four, to be less educated, to have fewer than eight years of formal schooling, and to be in lower-paying jobs; 44 percent are living below the poverty level, and 30 to 54 percent are likely to be Black or Hispanic.

Annual U.S. literacy rates are analyzed by several agencies. Depending upon how each identifies "illiteracy," the U.S. illiteracy percentages vary from 25 percent to 40 percent. Persons classified among the non-reading public share their memories in the oral tradition. Families with parents who rely on the oral tradition tend to use known dates or events to remember when an important family experience occurred.

Memories Surviving from Oral Traditions

Before 1865, oral tradition flourished among the U.S. slave population because few blacks could read; it was against the law to learn. However, *slave narratives* of memories of slavery are often expressed in the oral tradition. Some were recently performed in a theatrical venue and described by Steve Murray in a paradigm of memories (2003).

> Here are tales the likes of which you may have absorbed almost as folklore or the lyrics of a long ago, sad song. These experiences come to urgent, immediate life through the dramatic impersonations ("readings" is too dry a word for the result). A woman recalls being whipped as a child for eating a leftover biscuit, then having her wounds salted. Another describes her own conception: her mother's daylong rape by the three teenage sons of the plantation owner. Yet another remembers an attempted escape by another slave, a new mother who was torn from a tree and mutilated by the master's hounds. "Memories" summons a sense of extraordinary resilience. . . . In the end, the power of . . . memories lies equally in two terrifying realizations. First, of course, is the understanding of the miserable daily routine of muscle-tearing labor, cornmush-and-bean meals and physical/sexual abuse endured by these survivors of slavery. (E-1, E-4)

BEYOND SCHOOLING

As the general public tries to reach an understanding of the ultimate purpose of education, it is faced with a dilemma. In language that parents can understand, the choice that tends to surface is one between their children being prepared to enter the workplace or higher education.

Often, children from moderate- and low-income families are directed from high school graduation to work or a military career; high school graduates from middle-income families are directed toward state schools of higher education (Pullin 1994). These transitions are now made easier for school authorities through requirements associated with high-stakes testing.

Particular tests are called *high stakes* because failing these tests will determine whether a graduating student receives an *academic* or *nonacademic* diploma.

High-stakes tests are of two types: *criterion referenced* and *norm referenced* (Kubiszyn and Borich 2003). Criterion-referenced tests are designed to measure student performance based on criteria established by a state, city, or school district. Norm-referenced high-stakes tests are designed to measure the extent to which student performance matches the performance of students nationwide.

Policymakers often use standardized test scores to separate children from lower-income families from children in higher-income families. In the 1950s and '60s, it was common to place lower-income children into vocational pathways and their higher-income counterparts into academic pathways until parents organized against this wholesale practice.

Under the pretext of establishing a "high-skills" competitive workforce, politicians are campaigning for more standardized testing. These high-stakes tests are aligned with state requirements (often misnamed "standards") in the absence of any scientific evidence supporting their pronouncements that testing improves learning (Slack 1977).

One unfortunate result of the high-stakes environment has been that teachers are teaching to the test—thus creating a narrow curriculum to fit what the test purports to measure—while reducing the likelihood that children will be taught what all children need to know (Mitchell 1992; Wiggins 1998).

Too many school authorities, under local pressure, develop a formula that places students into two groups: children of color and children of lower-income non-black families in one group, and in the other are children of predominantly white and other upper-income families. Local social pressure on school authorities to establish separate pathways for these families is enormous. When a variety of social circumstances stands in the way of these separations, the solution is for upper-income families to enroll their children in private schools.

The quality of high schools is tightly tied to the economic level of the school district. Studies show that education in mathematics and in the physical sciences is particularly sensitive to the wealth of the school. The largest differences in teacher preparation between rich and poor schools are in mathematics, chemistry, and physics. The enormous disparities among high schools amplify rather than mediate the effects of differences in parental education and economic level. Because economic and ethnic/cultural lines are often correlated in the United States, inequities in the quality of high schools are a contributor to the differences between the population of scientists and the population of the country. Physical scientists are mostly white and mostly male. (Marshall, Scheppler, and Palmisano 2003, 25)

White families of modest income, often left alone with only their whiteness, have been trapped at a seldom-recognized social class level from which it is virtually impossible to advance. Their occupational choices start directly after completing high school or as a dropout. Their choices are limited to an occupation providing a modest income or a military career.

MEMORY AND RETRIEVAL
IN TODAY'S CLASSROOMS

In teaching and learning today, emphasis is placed upon what children should be taught, followed by a testing of retrieval. *How* children learn is seldom considered. The popular strategies in education today are designed to match what will be tested with the content to be taught. Schools purchase standardized curriculum and standardized tests, then proceed to standardized teaching of a content derived from previously introduced curricula (Slavin 2000).

Schooling in the United States continues to be problematic because experience, perception, attention, short-term memory (working memory), long-term memory, and retrieval are far too complex to be relegated to standardized teaching and testing (Pogrow 2002).

A set of complex problems tends to emerge when a single scripted and controlled system is used to educate thousands of students from different environments and among various social classes in hundreds of different school systems. Standardized curriculum and standardized tests are marketed to as many school districts as possible because they assume that "one size can fit all." Some programs are structured to the extent that even the phrasing to be used by the teacher is scripted.

One popular standardized program is called *Success for All*. This program is now being used in 1,500 schools in forty-eight states (Donsky 2003). Another well-known standardized program is *New American*

Schools. None have been successful in improving the performance of challenged readers (Pogrow 2002).

Rigidly structured programs have had some success in raising the test scores of some children. In today's education environment, the raising of test scores tends to outweigh more important knowledge-acquisition objectives. Reports on the program *Success for All* have been mixed, with some calling it ineffective (Pogrow 2002) while at the same time it is being defended by its marketers (Slavin 2002).

In today's education climate, school success rests completely on a performance that is rigidly designed for all learners.

Children who retrieve sufficient information from a standardized curriculum, and are able to do well on a paper-and-pencil standardized test designed to retrieve that information, tend to please many teachers, parents, and school administrators. Some teachers, however, are not sure that, following completion of school, their graduates will possess sufficient judgment and knowledge to share a successful life with colleagues and family above the lower levels of military service or modest occupations.

Allport, G. 1937. *Personality: A psychological interpretation.* New York: Henry Holt.

Altmann, E. M., and B. E. John. 1999. Episodic indexing: A model of memory for attention events. *Cognitive Science* 23: 117–56.

Apple, M. 1979. *Ideology and curriculum.* New York: Routledge and Kegan.

Apter, J. T. 1946. Eye movements following synchronization of the superior colliculus of cats. *Journal of Neurophysiology* 9, 73–86.

Atkinson, R. C., and R. M. Shiffrin. 1968. Human memory: A proposed system and its control processes. In *The psychology of learning and motivation: Advances in research and theory,* edited by K. W. Spence and J. T. Spence, 90–191. New York: Academic Press.

Baddeley, A. D. 1976. *The psychology of memory.* New York: Basic Books.

———. 1986. *Working memory.* Oxford: Oxford University Press.

———. 1990. *Human memory: Theory and practice.* Hillsdale, N.J.: Lawrence Erlbaum.

———. 1998. *Human memory: Theory and practice.* Boston, Mass.: Allyn and Bacon.

———. 1999. *Essentials of human memory.* East Sussex, U.K.: Psychology Press.

Bailey, G., and E. Thomas. 1998. Some aspects of African American vernacular English phonology. In *African American English: Structure, history, and use,* edited by J. Mufwene, G. Rickfod, G. Bailey, and J. Baugh, 85–109. London: Routledge.

Baldwin, J. 1963. *The fire next time.* New York: Dial Press.

Bandura, A. 1986. *Social foundations of thought and action: A social cognitive theory.* Englewood Cliffs, N.J.: Prentice Hall.

Bardouille-Crema, A. 1986. Performance on Piagetian tasks of black children of differing socioeconomic levels. *Developmental Psychology* 22, no. 6 (November): 841–44.

Barkley, R. A. 1981. *Hyperactive children: A handbook for diagnosis and treatment*. New York: Guildford.

———. 1990. *Attention-deficit hyperactivity disorder: A handbook for diagnosis and treatment*. New York: Guilford Press.

Beattie, G., and J. Coughlan. 1999. An experimental investigation of the role of iconic gestures in lexical access using the tip-of-the-tongue phenomenon. *British Journal of Psychology* 90, no. 1:35–56.

Beck, S. J. 1937. *Introduction to the Rorschach method*. New York: American Orthopsychiatric Association.

Benedict, R. 1959. *Race: Science and politics*. New York: Viking Press.

Bernal, M. 1987. *Black Athena: The Afroasiatic roots of classical civilization*. New Brunswick, N.J.: Rutgers University Press.

Bernard, M. E., and J. R. Joyce. 1984. *Rational-emotive therapy with children and adolescents: Theory, treatment strategies, and preventive methods*. New York: Wiley.

Binet, A., and Simon, T. 1916. *The development of intelligence in children*. Baltimore, Md.: Williams and Wilkins.

Blischak, D. M., and M. A. McDaniel. 1995. Effects of picture size and placement on memory for words. *Journal of Speech and Hearing Research* 38, no. 6: 1356–62.

Boas, F. 1974. *The shaping of American anthropology*. Chicago, Ill.: University of Chicago Press.

Bohannan, J. N., B. MacWinney, and C. E. Snow. 1990. Negative evidence revisited: Beyond learnability or who has to prove what to whom? *Developmental Psychology* 26: 221–26.

Borke, H. 1971. Interpersonal perception of young children: Egocentrism or empathy. *Developmental Psychology* 5, no. 2: 263–69.

Bower, T. G. R. 1971. The object in the world of the infant. *Scientific American* 225: 30–38.

Brentano, F. 1973. *Psychology from an empirical standpoint*. London: Routledge and Kegan Paul.

Broadbent, D. E. 1958. *Perception and communication*. London: Pergamon Press.

Bronfenbrenner, U. 1979. *The ecology of human development: Experiments by nature and design*. Cambridge, Mass.: Harvard University Press.

———. 1993. The ecology of cognitive development: Research models and fugitive findings. In *Development in context*, edited by R. W. Woznial and K. W. Fischer, 3–44. Hillsdale, N.J.: Lawrence Erlbaum.

———. 1995. The bioecological model from a life course perspective: Reflections of a participant observer. In *Examining lives in context*, edited by P. Moen, G. H. Elder Jr., and K. Luscher, 599–618. Washington, D.C.: American Psychological Association.

Bronfenbrenner, U., and S. J. Ceci. 1994. Nature-nurture reconceptualized in developmental perspective: A bioecological model. *Psychological Review* 101: 568–86.

Brown, R., and D. McNeill. 1966. The "tip of the tongue" phenomenon. *Journal of Verbal Learning and Verbal Behavior* 5: 325–37.

Brownowski, J. 1978. *The origins of knowledge and imagination*. New Haven, Conn.: Yale University Press.

Bruer, J. T. 1997. Education and the brain: A bridge too far. *Educational Researcher* 26, no. 8 (November): 4–16.

Bruner, J., R. R. Oliver, and P. M. Greenfield. 1966. *Studies in cognitive growth*. New York: Wiley.

Buckner, R. L., and D. Barch. 1999. Cognition: Memory, l: Episodic memory retrieval. *The American Journal of Psychiatry* 156, no. 9: 1311–32.

Buckner, R. L., S. E. Peterson, J. G. Ojemann, F. M. Miezin, L. R. Squire, and M. E. Raichle. 1995. Functional anatomical studies of explicit and implicit memory retrieval tasks. *Journal of Neuroscience* 15: 12–29.

Burnett, J. R. 1988. Dewey's educational thought and his mature philosophy. *Educational Theory* 38: 203–11.

Burnham, W. H. 1908. Attention and interest. *American Journal of Psychology* 19:14–18.

Burt, C. 1940. *Factors of the mind*. London: University of London Press.

———. 1957. Heredity and intelligence: A reply to criticisms. *British Journal of Statistical Psychology* 10: 33–63.

———. 1958. The inheritance of mental ability. *American Psychologist* 13: 1–15.

———. 1959. Class differences in general intelligence, III. *British Journal of Statistical Psychology* 14: 3–24.

———. 1966. The genetic determination of differences in intelligence: A study of monozygotic twins reared together and apart. *British Journal of Psychology* 57: 137–53.

Burt, C., and M. Howard. 1956. The multifactoral theory of inheritance and its application to intelligence. *British Journal of Statistical Psychology* 9: 95–131.

Byrnes, J. P. 2001. *Minds, brains, and learning: Understanding the psychological and educational relevance of neuroscientific research*. New York: Guilford Press.

Cahill, L., and J. L. McGaugh. 1996. Modulation of memory storage. *Current Opinion in Neurobiology* 6: 237–42.

Cermak, L. S. 1982. *Human memory and amnesia*. Hillsdale, N.J.: Lawrence Erlbaum.

Cherry, E. C. 1953. Some experiments on the recognition of speech, with one ear and with two ears. *Journal of the Acoustic Society of America*, 25: 975–979.

Chomsky, N. 1965. *Aspects of the theory of syntax*. Cambridge, Mass.: MIT Press.

———. 1968. *Language and mind*. New York: Harcourt, Brace and World.

———. 1976. *Reflections on language*. New York: Pantheon.

———. 2001. *9/11*. New York: Seven Stories Press.

Christel, M. 1993. Grasping techniques and hand preferences hominoidea. In *Hands of primates*, edited by H. Preuschoft and D. H. Chivers, 98–108. New York: Springer-Verlig.

Christianson, S. A., ed. 1992. *Handbook of emotion and memory: Current research and theory*. Hillsdale, N.J.: Lawrence Erlbaum.

Church, B. A., and D. L. Schacter. 1994. Perceptual specificity of auditory priming: Implicit memory for voice intonation and fundamental frequency. *Journal of Experimental Psychology: Learning Memory and Cognition* 20: 521–53.

Cohen, M. R., and S. Scheer. 1997. *The work of teachers in America: A social history through stories*. Mahwah, N.J.: Erlbaum.

Cohen, N. J., G. Weiss, and K. Minde. 1972. Cognitive styles in adolescents previously diagnosed as hyperactive. *Journal of Child Psychology and Psychiatry* 13: 203–9.

Cooper, R. P., and R. N. Aslin. 1990. Preference for infant-directed speech in the first month after birth. *Child Development* 61: 1584–95.

Cornwell, J. M. & Manfredo, P. A. (1994). Kolb's learning style theory revisited. *Educational and Psychological Measurement* (54) 2, 317–328.

Cowey, A., and P. Stoerig. 1995. Blindsight in monkeys. *Nature*: 373, 247–249.

Craik, F. I. M., and R. L. Lockhart. 1972. Levels of processing: A framework for memory research. *Journal of Verbal Learning and Verbal Behavior* 11: 671–84.

Dalgleish, T., and M. J. Power. 1999. *Handbook of cognition and emotion*. New York: Wiley.

Daneman, M. & Tardif, T. 1987. Working memory and recall skill reexamined. In M. Caltheart (Ed.) Attention and Performance. *The Psychology of Reading*, 12, 491–508. Hove: Lawrence Erlbaum Associates.

Danquah, J. B. 1927. Foreword in *United West Africa or Africa at the bar of the family of nations*, edited by S. Lapido, 3–5. London: African Publication Society.

Dasen, P. R. 1978. *Piagetian psychology: Cross-cultural contributions*. New York: Gardner Press.

DeCato, C. M. and Z. A. Piotrowski. 1977. *A concise manual for Rorschach interpretation*. Cherry Hill, NJ: Post Graduate International.

Deese, J., and S. H. Hulse. 1967. *The psychology of learning*. New York: Mc-Graw-Hill.

Denton, D. ed. 1974. *Existentialism and phenomenology of education: Collected essays*. New York: Teachers College Press.

Deutsch, J. A., and D. Deutsch. 1963. Attention: Some theoretical considerations. *Psychological Review* 70: 80–90.

Dewey, J. 1897. My pedagogic creed. *The School Journal* 54, no. 3: 77–80.

———. 1933. *How we think*. Boston: Heath.

Dixon, R. A., and C. Hertzog. 1988. A functional approach to memory and metamemory in adulthood. In *Memory development: Universal changes and universal differences*, edited by F. W. Weinert and M. Perlmutter, 3–30. Hillsdale, N.J.: Erlbaum.

Donsky, P. 2003. Lesson programs lift schools' hopes. *Atlanta Journal Constitution*, February 16: C2, C9.

Dorfman, D. D. 1978. The Cyril Burt question: New findings. *Science* 201, no. 4362 (September): 1177–86.

Dreyfus, H. L., and H. Hall, eds. 1982. *Husserl: Intentionality and cognitive science*. Cambridge, Mass.: MIT Press.

Dunn, R., & Dunn, K. (1978). *Teaching students through their individual learning styles: A practical approach*. Reston, VA: Reston Publishing Company.

Durso, F. T., and M. K. Johnson. 1980. The effects of orienting tasks on recognition recall and modality confusion of pictures and words. *Journal of Verbal Learning and Verbal Behavior* 19: 416–29.

Ebbinghaus, H. 1885. *Memory: A contribution to experimental psychology*, trans. by H. A. Ruger and C. E. Bussenius, with a new introduction by E. R. Hilgard. Reprint, New York: Dover, 1964.

Egeland, B. 1974. Training impulsive children in the use of more efficient scanning techniques. *Child Development* 45: 165–71.

Eliot, C. W. 1909. *Folk-lore and fable: Aesop, Grimm, Anderson*. New York: Collier and Son. Reprint, 1969.

Elkind, D., R. R. Koegler, and E. Go. 1962. Effects of perceptual training at three age levels. *Science* 137, no. 3532: 755–56.

Ellis, A. 1971. *Humanistic psychotherapy.* New York: Crown.

Ellis, A., and J. M. Whitely. 1979. *Theoretical and empirical foundations of rational-emotive therapy.* Monterey, Calif.: Brooks/Cole.

Engelkamp, J., and H. D. Zimmer. 1994. *The human memory: A multimodal approach.* Seattle, Wash.: Hogrefe and Huber.

Ericsson, K. A. 2000. Some shortcomings of long-term working memory. *British Journal of Psychology* 91, no. 4: 571–90.

Ericsson, K. A., and W. Kintsch. 1995. Long-term working memory. *Psychological Review* 102: 211–45.

———. W. 2000. Shortcomings of generic retrieval structures with slots of the type that Gobet proposed and modelled. *British Journal of Psychology* 91, 571–590.

Estes, W. K., and H. A. Taylor. 1966. Visual detection in relation to display size and redundancy of critical elements. *Perception and Psychophysics* 1: 9–16.

Eysenck, M. W., and A. Byrne. 1994. Implicit memory bias, explicit memory bias, and anxiety. *Cognition and Emotion* 8: 415–31.

Fadiga, L., L. Fogassi, G. Pavesi, and Rizzoliti 1995. Motor facilitation during action observation: A magnetic stimulation study. *Journal of Neurophysiology* 73, 2608–11.

Fancher, R. E. 1985. *The intelligence men: Makers of the IQ controversy.* New York: Norton.

Farah, M. 1989. The neural basis of mental imagery. *Trends in Neuroscience* 12: 395–99.

Farley, R., and W. R. Allen. 1987. *The color line and the quality of life in America.* New York: Russell Sage Foundation.

Fechner, G. 1860. *Elements of psychophysics*, vol. 1, translated by H. E. Adler and edited by D. H. Howes and E. G. Boring, with an introduction by E. G. Boring. Reprint, New York: Holt, Rinehart and Winston, 1966.

Feinberg, W. 1998. Rejoinder: Meaning, pedagogy, and curriculum development. *Educational Researcher* (October): 30–37.

Fernald, A. 1989. Intonation and communicative intent in mothers' speech to infants: Is the melody the message? *Child Development* 60: 1497–510.

Fitts, P. M. 1954. The information capacity of the human motor system in controlling the amplitude of movement. *The Journal of Experimental Psychology* 47: 381–91.

Freedman, R. D., & Stumpf, S. A. (1978). What can one learn from the learning style inventory? *Academy of Management Journal* (21) 2, 275–282.

Freedman, R. D., & Stumpf, S. A. (1980). Learning style theory: Less than meets the eye. *Academy of Management Review* (5) 3, 445–447.

Freire, P. 1972. *Pedagogy of the oppressed*. New York: Penguin Books.

Freud, S. 1954. *The origins of psychoanalysis: Letters to Wilhelm Fliess*. New York: Basic Books.

Fuld, P. A. 1976. Storage, retention, and retrieval in Korsakoff's syndrome. *Neuropsychologia* 14: 225–36.

Gabrieli, J. D., M. M. Fleischman, S. L. Keane, S. L. Reminger, and F. Morrell. 1995. Double dissociation between memory systems underlying explicit and implicit memory in the human brain. *Psychological Science* 6: 76–82.

Gamer, L. (2000). Problems and inconsistencies with Kolb's learning styles. *Educational Psychology*, (20) 3, 341–349.

Gardner, H. 1983. *Frames of mind*. New York: Basic Books.

———. 1987. The theory of multiple intelligence. *Annals of Dyslexia* 37, 33–35.

Gary, M., and D. J. L. Polaschek. 2000. Imagination and memory. *Journal of the American Psychological Society* 9, no. 1: 6–10.

Gesell, A. 1949. *Gesell developmental schedules*. New York: Psychological Corp.

Ghent, L. 1956. Perception of overlapping and embedded figures by children of different ages. *American Journal of Psychology* 69, no. 4: 575–87.

Gibson, E. J. 1963. Perceptual development. In *Child psychology: Sixty-second yearbook of the society for the study of education*. Part 1, edited by Harold W. Stevenson, 144–95. Chicago, Ill.: University of Chicago Press.

———. 1965. Learning to read. *Science* 148, no. 3673: 1066–72.

Gibson, J. J. 1966. *The senses considered as perceptual systems*. Boston: Houghton Mifflin.

Ginsburg, H., and S. Opper. 1969. *Piaget's theory of intellectual development*. Englewood Cliffs, N.J.: Prentice Hall.

Gobet, F. 2000a. Long-term working memory: A computational implementation for chess expertise. Proceedings of the third international conference on cognitive modeling, 142–49. Veenendaal, The Netherlands: Universal Press.

———. 2000b. Some shortcomings of long-term working memory. *British Journal of Psychology* 91: 551–70.

Gobet, F., and H. A. Simon. 1998. Expert chess memory: Revisiting the chunking hypothesis. *Memory* 6: 225–55.

Goodale, M. A. 1983. Neural mechanisms of visual orientation in rodents: Targets versus places. In *Spatially oriented behavior,* edited by A. Hein and M. Jeannerod. New York: Springer-Verlag.

Goodenough, F. F. 1949. *Mental testing*. New York: Rinehart.

Gould, S. J. 1977. *Ever since Darwin: Reflections in natural history*. New York: Norton.

———. 1980. *The panda's thumb: More reflections in natural history*. New York: Norton.

———. 1981. *The mismeasure of man*. New York: Norton.

———. 1983. *Hen's teeth and horse's toes*. New York: Norton.

———. 2002. *The structure of evolutionary theory*. Boston, Mass.: Harvard University Press.

Gratch, G. 1975. Recent studies based on Piaget's view of object concept development. In *Infant perception: From sensation to cognition*, vol. 2, edited by L. B. Cohen and P. Salapatek. New York: Academic Press.

Greene, M. 1973. *Teacher as stranger: Educational philosophy for the modern age*.

———. 1978. *Landscapes of learning*. New York: Columbia University Press.

———. 1986. In search of a critical pedagogy. *Harvard Educational Review* 56: 424–41.

———. 1988. *The dialectic of freedom*. New York: Teachers College Press.

Grolnick, W. S., and M. L. Slowiaczek. 1994. Parents' involvement of children's schooling; A multidimensional conceptualization and motivational model. *Child Development* 65: 237–52.

Guthrie, E. R. 1935. *The psychology of learning*. New York: Harper and Row.

———. 1952. *The psychology of learning*. Rev. ed. New York: Harper and Row.

Hacker, A. 1994, October. White on white. *The New Republic*, 13–14.

Haley, J. 1972. Family therapy. In *Progress in group and family therapy*, edited by C. J. Sager and H. S. Kaplan. New York: Bruner/Mazel.

Halgren, E., and K. Marinkovic. 1995. Neurophysical networks integrating human emotions. In *The cognitive neuroscience*, edited by M. S. Gazzaniga, 1137–51. Cambridge, Mass.: MIT Press.

Harley, R., and G. A. Lawrence. 1984. *Visual impairment in the schools*. Springfield, Ill.: Charles Thomas.

Hart, B., and T. R. Risley. 1995. *Meaningful differences in the everyday experience of young American children*. Baltimore, Md.: Brookes

Hasher, L., and R. T. Zacks. 1979. Automatic and effortful processes in memory. *Journal of Experimental Psychology* 108: 556–88.

Hebb, D. O. 1949. *The organization of behavior*. New York: Wiley.

———. 1955. Drives and the central nervous system. *Psychological Review* 62: 243–54.

———. 1958. *A textbook on psychology*. Philadelphia: Sanders.

———. 1959. A neuropsychological theory. In *Psychology: A study of science*, vol. 1, edited by S. Koch. New York: McGraw Hill.

————. 1966. *A textbook on psychology*. Philadelphia: Sanders.

————. 1972. *A textbook on psychology*. Philadelphia: Sanders.

Hechinger, F. M. 1979. About education: Further proof that I.Q. data were fraudulent. *New York Times*, January 30: C4.

Heffner, R., and B. Masterton. 1975. Variation in form of the pyramidal tract and its relationship to digital dexterity. *Brain, Behavior, and Evolution* 12: 1612–2000.

Heidegger, M. 1962. *Being and time*. London: SCM Press.

Heider, E. R. 1971. Information processing and the modification of an impulsive conceptual tempo. *Child Development* 42: 1276–81.

Hein, A., and R. Held. 1967. Disassociation of the visual placing response into elicited and guided components. *Science* 158: 190–92.

Henry, J. 1965. *Culture against man*. New York: Vintage Books.

Herbert, J. 2000. Memory retrieval by eighteen- to thirty-month-olds: Age related changes in representational flexibility. *Developmental Psychology* 36, no. 4: 473–84.

Herrnstein, R. J. 1973. *IQ and meritocracy*. Boston: Little, Brown.

Herrnstein, R. J., and C. Murray. 1994. *The bell curve: Intelligence and class structure in American life*. New York: Free Press.

Heuer, H., and A. F. Sanders, eds. 1987. *Perceptions on perspective and action*. Hillsdale, N.J.: Lawrence Erlbaum.

Higgins, A. T., and J. E. Turnure. 1984. Distractibility and concentration of attention in children's development. *Child Development* 55: 1799–810.

Hirsch, E. D. 1993. *What your sixth grader needs to know: Fundamentals of a good sixth-grade education*. New York: Doubleday.

———— 1996. *The schools we need and why we don't have them*. New York: Doubleday.

Holt, J. 1976. *Instead of education*. New York: Dutton.

Husserl, E. 1913. *Ideas pertaining to a pure phenomenology and to phenomenological philosophy*. Reprint, Martinus Nijhoff: The Hague, 1982.

————. 1929. *Cartesian meditations*. Reprint, Martinus Nijhoff: The Hague, 1965.

Irwin-Chase, H., and B. Burns. 2000. Developmental changes in children's abilities to share and allocate attention in a dual task. *Journal of Experimental Child Psychology* 77, no. 1: 61–85.

Itzkoff, S. W. 1994. *The decline of intelligence in America*. Westport, Conn.: Praeger.

Jacoby, L., and D. Witherspoon. 1982. Remembering without awareness. *Canadian Journal of Psychology* 36: 300–24.

Jaffe, J., D. Stern, and C. Perry. 1973. "Conversational" coupling of gaze behavior in prelinguistic human development. *Journal of Psycholinguistic Research* 2: 321–30.

James, W. 1890. *The principles of psychology.* New York: Henry Holt and Company. Reprinted by Dover Publications in 1950.

Jankowski, J. J., S. A. Rose, and J. F. Feldman. 2001. Modifying the distribution of attention in infants. *Child Development* 27, no. 2: 339–51.

Jaspers, K. 1969–1971. *Philosophy.* 3 vols. Chicago, Ill.: University of Chicago Press.

Jeannerod, M. 1981. Intersegmental coordination during reaching at natural visual objects. In *Attention and performance*, edited by J. Long and A. Baddeley. Hillsdale, N.J.: Erlbaum.

Jensen, A. R. 1969. How much can we boost IQ? *Harvard Educational Review,* 3: 1–123.

Jung, C. G. 1915: Studies in word association. New York: Moffat Yard.

————. 1921. Psychological types. Trans. H. G. Bayles, revised 1971 by R. F. C. Hull. Princeton, N.J.: Princeton University Press.

Kahneman, D. 1973. *Attention and effort.* Englewood Cliffs, NJ: Prentice Hall.

Kamin, L. 1974. *The science and politics of I.Q.* Potomac, Md.: Lawrence Erlbaum.

————. 1995. Behind the curve. *Scientific American* 272, no. 2 (February): 99–104.

————. 1996. Explaining the fluctuation in black student test scores. *Journal of Blacks in Higher Education* 10: 98–99.

Kamin, L., and W. P. Isham. 1993. Blackness, deafness, IQ, and "g." *Intelligence* 17: 37–46.

Kaufman, A. S. 1992. Evaluation of the WISC-III and WIPPSI-R for gifted children. *Roeper Review* (March): 156–60.

Keele, S. W. 1973. *Attention and human performance.* Pacific Palisades, Calif.: Goodyear.

Kephart, N. C. 1960. *The slow learner in the classroom.* Columbus, Oh.: Merrill.

Kersten, A. W., and L. B. Smith. 2002. Attention to novel objects during verb learning. *Child Development* 73, no. 1: 93–109

Kett, J., J. Trefil, and J. Hirsch. 1987. *Cultural literacy: What every American needs to know.* Boston: Houghton Mifflin

Kierkegaard, S. 1941. *Fear and trembling.* Princeton, N.J.: Princeton University Press.

Klatzky, R. L. 1984. *Memory and awareness: An information processing perspective.* New York: Freeman.

Klein, J. 2001. Attention, scholastic achievement, and timing of lessons. *Scandinavian Journal of Educational Research* 45, no. 3: 301–9.

Klopfer, B., and D. M. Kelly. 1942. *The Rorschach technique.* Yonkers-on-Hudson, N.Y.: World Book.

Koffka, K. 1925. *The growth of the mind.* New York: Harcourt, Brace, and World.

———. 1935. *Principles of Gestalt psychology.* New York: Harcourt, Brace, and World.

Kohler, W. 1927. *The mentality of apes.* New York: Harcourt, Brace, and World.

———. 1929. *Gestalt psychology.* New York: Liveright.

Kolb, D. A. (1976). *Learning style inventory: Technical manual.* Englewood Cliffs, NJ: Prentice Hall.

Kolb, D. A. (1984). *Experiential learning: Experience as a source of learning development.* Englewood Cliffs, NJ: Prentice Hall

Kolb, D. A. (1985). *Learning style inventory: Self-scoring inventory and interpretation booklet.* Boston, MA: McBer & Company.

Kostelnik, M. J., L. C. Stein, A. P. Whiren, and A. K. Soderman. 1998. *Guiding children's social development: Classroom practices.* Albany, N.Y.: Delmar.

Kubiszyn, T., and G. Borich. 2003. *Education testing and measurement.* New York: Wiley.

Labov, W. 2001. *Principles of linguistic change: Social factors.* Vol. 2. Malden, Mass.: Blackwell.

Landau, S., E. P. Lorch, and R. Milich. 1992. Visual attention and comprehension of television in attention-deficit hyperactivity disorder and normal boys. *Child Development* 63: 928–37.

Lane, R., L. Nadel, and G. Ahern. 2000. *Cognitive neuroscience of emotion.* New York: Oxford University Press.

Larkin, M. 2000. Steering clear of tip-of-the-tongue experiences. *The Lancet* 356, no. 9243: 1743–44.

Laufer, N. W. 1962. Cerebral dysfunction and behavior disorders in adolescents. *American Journal of Orthopsychiatry* 32: 501–6.

Lawson, A. E., & Johnson, M. (2002). The validity of Kolb learning styles and neoPiagetian development levels in college biology. *Studies in Higher Education* 27(1), 79–90.

Lehrer, K. 2000. *Theory of knowledge.* Boulder, Colo.: Westview Press.

Lenneberg, E. 1967. *Biological foundations of language.* New York: Wiley.

Lewin, K. 1951. *Field theory in social science.* New York: Harper and Row.

Linn, R. L., E. L. Baker, and D. W. Betebenner. 2002. Accountability systems:

Implications of requirements of the No Child Left Behind Act of 2001. *Educational Researcher* 31, no. 6: 3–16.

Mack, A., E. Tang, R. Tuma, S. Kahn, and I. Rock. 1992. Perceptual organization and attention. *Cognitive Psychology* 24: 475–501.

Margalit, A. 2002. *The ethics of memory.* Cambridge, Mass.: Harvard University Press.

Marshall, S. P., J. A. Scheppler, and M. J. Palmisano, eds. 2003. *Science literacy for the twenty-first century.* New York: Prometheus Books.

Masataka, N. 1993. Effects of contingent and noncontingent maternal stimulation on the vocal behavior of three- to four-year-old Japanese infants. *Journal of Child Language* 20: 303–12.

McDowall, J. 1981. Effects of encoding instructions and retrieval cuing on recall in amount of work. *Journal of Experimental Psychology* 42: 82–93.

McGaugh, J. L., and M. J. Herz. 1972. *Memory consolidation.* San Francisco: Albion.

Mead, M. 1955. *Childhood in contemporary culture.* Chicago, Ill.: University of Chicago Press.

Medina, N., and M. Neill. 1990. *Fallout from the testing explosion: How 100 million standardized exams undermine excellence and equity in America's public schools.* Cambridge, Mass.: Fair Test.

Meichenbaum, D. H., and J. Goodman. 1969. Reflection-impulsivity and verbal control of motor behavior. *Child Development* 40: 785–97.

Melton, A. W. 1963. Implications of short-term memory for a general theory of memory. *Journal of Verbal Learning and Verbal Behavior* 2: 1–21.

Menkes, M. M., J. S. Rowe, and J. H. Menkes. 1967. A twenty-five year follow-up study on the hyperkinetic child with minimal brain dysfunction. *Pediatrics* 39: 393–99.

Meredith, R. A. 1978. Improved oral test scores through delayed response. *Modern Language Journal* 62: 321–27.

Milner, P. M. 1957. The cell assembly: Mark ll. *Psychological Review* 64: 242–52.

Mischel, H. N., and W. Mischel. 1983. Development of children's knowledge of self-control strategies. *Child Development* 54, 603–19.

Mischel, W. 1973. Towards a cognitive social learning conceptualization of personality. *Psychological Review* 80: 252–83.

———. 1974. Process in the delay of gratification. In *Advances in experimental social psychology.* Vol. 7, edited by L. Berkowitz, 249–92. New York: Academic Press.

Mischel, W., and E. Ebbesen. Attention in delay of gratification. *Journal of Personality and Social Psychology* 21: 204–18.

Mitchell, R. 1992. *Testing for learning: How new approaches to education can improve American Schools*. Cambridge, Mass.: Fair Test.

Montagu, A. 1999. *Race & IQ: Expanded edition*. New York: Oxford University Press.

Montgomery, K. C. 1951. Spontaneous attention as a function of time between trials and schooling: A multidimensional conceptualization and motivational model. *Child Development* 65: 237–52.

Moores, D. 1987. *Educating the deaf: Psychology, principles, and practices*. Boston: Houghton Mifflin.

Morgan, C. D., and H. A. Murray. 1935. A method for investigating fantasies: The Thematic Apperception Test. *Archives of Neurological Psychiatry* 34: 289–306.

Morgan, H. 1996. An analysis of Gardner's theory of multiple intelligences. *Roeper Review* 18, no. 4: 263–69.

———. 1997. *Cognitive styles and classroom learning*. Westport, Conn: Praeger.

———. 1999. *The imagination of early childhood education*. Westport, Conn.: Bergin and Garvey.

Morgan, J. 1990. Input, innateness, and induction in language acquisition. *Developmental Psychology* 23: 661–78.

Morris, N., and D. M. Jones. 1990. Memory updating in working memory: The role of the central executive. *British Journal of Psychology* 81, no. 2: 111–19.

Morris, V. C. 1966. *Existentialism in education: What it means*. New York: Harper and Row.

Moscovitch, M. 1982. Multiple dissociations of function in amnesia. In *Human memory and amnesia*, edited by L. Cermak. Hillsdale, N.J.: Lawrence Erlbaum.

Murray, S. 2003. HBO offers personal view of the horrors of slavery. *Atlanta Journal-Constitution*, February 10: E1, E4.

Myers, I. B., and P. B. Briggs. 1980: *Gifts differing*. Palo Alto, Calif.: Consulting Psychologist Press.

Myers, I. B., and M. H. McCaulley. 1985. Manual: A guide to the development and use of the Myers-Briggs Type Indicator. Palo Alto, Calif.: Consulting Psychologist Press.

Nairne, J. S. 2002. Remembering over the short term: The case against the standard model. *Annual Review of Psychology* 53: 53–81.

Napier, J. R. 1961. Prehensility and opposability in the hands of primates. *Symposium of the Zoology Society*: London, 5: 115–132.

Neisser, U. 1982. *Memory observed*. San Francisco, Calif.: W. H. Freeman.

Nelson, T. O., J. Metzler, and D. A. Reed. 1974. Role of details in long-term recognition of pictures and verbal descriptions. *Journal of Experimental Psychology* 102: 184–86.

Neugroschel, J. 2001. *The complete short stories of Marcel Proust*. New York: First Cooper Square Press.

Nigl, A., and W. Fishbein. 1974. Perception and conception in coordination and perspectives. *Developmental Psychology* 10, no. 6: 858–66.

Nino, A. 1979. Piaget's theory of space perception in infancy. *Cognition* 7, no. 2: 125–44.

Norman, D. A. 1976. *Memory and attention: An introduction to human information processing*. 2nd ed. New York: Wiley.

Norman, D. A., and T. Shallice. 1986. *Attention to action: Willed and automatic control of behavior*. Rockville, Md.: National Institute of Mental Health. ED 205562.

Nussbaum, M. C. 2001. *Upheavals of thought: The intelligence of emotions*. New York: Cambridge University Press.

Oakhill, J. V. 1984. Inferential and memory skills in children's comprehension of stories. *British Journal of Educational Psychology* 54: 31–39.

Paivio, A., and K. Csapo. 1973. Picture superiority in free recall: Imagery or dual coding? *Cognitive Psychology* 5: 176–206.

Parault, S. J., and P. J. Schwanenflugel. 2000. The development of conceptual categories of attention during the elementary school years. *Journal of Experimental Child Psychology* 75, no. 4: 245–62.

Pashler, H. E. 1998. *The psychology of attention*. Boston, Mass.: MIT Press.

Pellegrino, J. W., A. W. Siegel, and M. Dhawan. 1976. Short-term versions of pictures and words as a function of type of distraction and length of delay interval. *Memory and Cognition* 4: 11–15.

Perrig, P., and D. Hofer. 1989. Sensory and conceptual representations in memory: Motor images which cannot be imagined. *Psychological Research* 5: 201–7.

Piaget, J. 1954. *The construction of reality in the child*. New York: Free Press.

———. 1971. *The language and thought of the child*. New York: World Publishing. (Original work published 1926)

———. 1969. *The psychology of the child*. New York: Basic Books.

Piaget, J., and B. Inhelder. 1948. *The child's conception of space*, trans. by F. J. Langdon and J. L. Lunzer. London: Rutledge and Kegan Paul.

———. 1969. *The psychology of the child*. New York: Basic Books.

Pick, A. D. 1965. Improvement of visual and tactual form discrimination. *Journal of Experimental Psychology* 69, no. 4: 331–39.

Pillsbury, W. B. 1897. A study in perception. *American Journal of Psychology* 8: 315–93.

Pinker, S. 1994. *The language instinct: How the mind creates language.* New York: William Morrow.

Pliszka, S. R. 2003. *Neuroscience for the mental health clinician.* New York: Guilford Press.

Pogrow, S. 2002. Success for all is a failure. *Phi Delta Kappan* 83, no. 6: 463–68.

Polyak, S. 1957. *The vertebrate visual system.* Chicago, Ill.: University of Chicago Press.

Posner, M. I., and S. E. Peterson. 1990. The attention system of the human brain. *Annual Review of Cognitive Neuroscience* 13: 24–42.

Prizant, B. M., and A. M. Wetherby. 1990. Toward an integrated view of early language and communication development and socioemotional development. *Topics in Language Disorders* 10: 1–16.

Pullin, D. C. 1994. Learning to work: The impact of curriculum assessment standards on educational opportunity. *Harvard Educational Review* 64, no. 1.

Reiff, R., and M. Scheerer. 1959. *Memory and hypnotic age regression.* New York: New York International Universities Press.

Rensberger, B. 1976. Briton's classic IQ data now viewed as fraudulent. *New York Times*, November 28: 9

Rensberger, B. 1978. Data on race role in IQ called false. *New York Times*, November 8: 9.

Reynolds, M. 1997. Learning styles: A critique. *Management learning*, 28 (2), 115–133

Ribot, T. A. 1882. *Diseases of memory.* New York: Appleton.

Riding, R. J., Grimley, M., Dahraei, H., & Banner, G. (2003). Cognitive style, working memory and learning behavior and attainment in school subjects. *British Journal of Educational Psychology*, 73, 2, 149–170.

Riding, R. J., & Calvey, L. 1981. The assessment of verbal-imagery learning styles and their effect on the recall of concrete and abstract passages by eleven year old children. *British Journal of Psychology* 72, 59–64.

Ritchie, W., and T. Bhatia. 1999: Child language development: Introduction, foundations, and overview. In *Handbook of child language acquisition*, edited by W. Ritchie and T. Bhatia, 1–33. New York: Academic Press.

Robinson, P. 1995. Attention, memory, and the noticing hypothesis. *Language Learning* 45, no. 2: 283–331.

Rock, I. 1984. *Perception.* New York: Freeman.

Roediger, H. L. 1990. Implicit memory: Retention without remembering. *American Psychologist* 45: 1043–56.

Rogers, J. A. 1972. *World's great men of color.* New York: Collier Books.

Rose, S. A., J. F. Feldman, and J. J. Jankowski. 2001. Attention and recognition memory in the first year of life: A longitudinal study of preterm and full-term infants. *Developmental Psychology* 37, no. 1: 135–51.

Ruff, H. A., and M. K. Rothbart. 1996. *Attention in early development.* New York: Oxford University Press.

Ryan, S. 1993. The Panama deception. *Cineaste* 20, no. 1 (winter): 43.

Sachs, J. 1977. The adaptive significance of linguistic input to prelinguistic infants. In *Talking to children*, edited by C. Snow and C. A. Ferguson. New York: Cambridge University Press.

Saffran, J. R., R. Griepentrog, and J. Gregory. 2001. Absolute pitch in infant auditory learning: Evidence for development reorganization. *Developmental Psychology* 37, no. 1: 74–85.

Saffran, J. R., M. M. Loman, M. Michelle, and R. W. Robertson. 2000. Infant memory for musical experiences. *Cognition* 77, no. 1 (October 16): B15–23.

Sager, C. J., and H. Kaplan. 1972. *Progress in group and family therapy.* New York: Brunner/Mazel.

Schachar, R., and G. D. Logan. 1990. Impulsivity and inhibitory control in normal development and child psychopathology, *Developmental Psychology* 26, no. 5: 710–20.

Schachar, R. and L. Gordon. 1990. Are hyperactive children deficient in attentional capacity? *Journal of Abnormal Child Psychology*, 18: 5, 493–512.

Schachar, R., M. Rutter, and A. Smith. 1981. The characteristics of situationally and pervasively hyperactive children: Implications for syndrome definition. *Journal of Child Psychology and Psychiatry* 22, no. 4: 375–92.

Schacter, D. L., and R. L. Buckner. 1998. Priming the brain. *Neuron* 20: 185–95.

Schiff, W., and C. I. Saarni. 1976. Perception and conservation of length: Piaget and Taponier revisited. *Child Development* 47, no. 2: 427–33.

Schrag, P., and D. Divoky. 1975. *The myth of the hyperactive child: And other means of child control.* New York: Pantheon Books.

Schwartz, F. D. 2003. The oldest talkie. *Invention & Technology* (spring): 10.

Shacter, H. S. 1933. A method for measuring the sustained attention of preschool children. *Journal of Genetic Psychology* 42: 339–69.

Shaffer, D. 1994. Attention deficit hyperactivity disorder in adults. *American Journal of Psychiatry* 151: 633–38.

Shafto, M., ed. 1985. *How we know.* New York: Harper and Row.

Shah, P., & Miyake, A. 1996. The separability of working memory resources for spatial thinking and language processing: An individual differences approach. *Journal of Experimental Psychology: General*, 125, 4–27.

Shallice, T. 1974. On the contents of primary memory. In *Attention and performance*. Vol. 5, edited by P. M. A. Rabbit and S. Dornic. London: Academic Press.

———. 1988. *From neuropsychology to mental structure*. New York: Oxford University Press.

Sheingold, K. 1973, August. Developmental differences in intake and storage of visual information. *Journal of Experimental Child Psychology*, 16: 1, 1–11.

Shiffrin, R. M., and W. Schneider. 1977. Controlled and automatic human information processing: Part 2. Perceptual learning, automatic attending, and general theory. *Psychological Review* 84: 127–90.

Sigel, I. E., and F. H. Hooper. 1968. *Logical thinking in children: Research based on Piaget's theory*. New York: Holt, Rinehart and Winston.

Skinner, B. F. 1953. *Science and human behavior*. New York: Macmillan.

———. 1957. *Verbal behavior*. New York: Appleton-Century-Crofts.

———. 1974. *About behaviorism*. New York: Vintage.

Sklar, H. 2003. Gaps between black and white still wide. *Atlanta Journal-Constitution*, January 17: A15.

Slack, W. V. 1977. Firmly against SATs. *New York Times*, November 19: 21.

Slavin, R. E. 2000. Putting the school back in school reform. *Educational Leadership* 58, no. 4: 22–27.

———. 2002. Mounting evidence supports the achievement effects of success for all. *Phi Delta Kappan* 83, no. 6: 469–71.

Snowden, F. M. 1970. *Blacks in antiquity*. Cambridge, Mass.: Harvard University Press.

Solan, H. A., S. Larson, J. Shelly-Trembly, A. Ficarra, and M. Silverman. 2001. Role of visual attention in cognitive control of oculomotor readiness in students with reading disabilities. *Journal of Learning Disabilities* 34, no. 2: 107–18.

Sonuga-Barke, E. J. S., K. Houlberg, and M. Hall. 1994. When is "impulsiveness" not impulsive? The case of hyperactive children's cognitive style. *Journal of Child Psychology and Psychiatry* 35, no. 7: 1247–53.

Sonuga-Barke, E. J. S., and E. Taylor. 1992. The effects of delay on hyperactive and non-hyperactive children's response times: A research note. *Journal of Child Psychology and Psychiatry* 33, no. 6: 1091–96.

Spearman, C. 1904. General intelligence objectively determined and measured. *American Journal of Psychology* 15: 201–93.

Sperling, G. 1967. Successive approximations to a model for short-term memory. *Acta Psychologica* 27: 285–92.

Spieth, W., J. F. Curtis, and J. C. Webster. 1954. Responding to one of two simultaneous messages. *Journal of the Acoustical Society of America* 26: 391–96.

Squire, L. R. 1984. *Memory and brain*. New York: Oxford University Press.

Squire, L. R., and N. Butters. 1984. *Neuropsychology of memory*. New York: Guilford Press.

Taylor, R. L., and S. B. Richards. 1991. Patterns of intellectual differences of Black, Hispanic, and White children. *Diagnostique* 17: 49–56.

Techner, E. B. 1908. *Lectures on the elementary psychology of feeling and attention*. New York: Macmillan.

Terman, L. M., and M. A. Merrill. 1937. *Measuring intelligence*. Boston: Houghton Mifflin.

Thorndike, E. L. 1913. *The psychology of learning*. New York: Teacher's College

Thurstone, L. L. 1938. *Primary mental abilities*. Chicago, Ill.: University of Chicago.

———. 1946. *Tests of primary mental abilities for ages five and six*. Chicago, Ill.: Science Research Associates.

Towse, J. N. 1998. On random generation and the central executive of working memory. *British Journal of Psychology* 89, no. 1: 77–101.

Trabasso, T., and H. B. Bower. 1968. *Attention in learning: Theory and research*. New York: Wiley and Sons

Treisman, A. M. 1960. Contextual clues in selective attention. *Quarterly Journal of Experimental Psychology* 12: 242–48.

———. 1969. Strategies and models of selective attention. *Psychological Review* 76: 282–99.

———. 1977. Focused attention in the perception and retrieval of multidimensional stimuli. *Perception and Psychophysics* 22, no. 1: 1–11.

Tulving, E. 1972. Episodic and semantic memory. In *Organization of memory*, edited by E. Tulving and W. Donaldson. New York: Academic Press.

———. 1992. Ebbinghaus, Hermann. In *Encyclopedia of learning and memory*, edited by L. R. Squire. New York: Macmillan.

———. Episodic memory: From mind to brain. *Annual Review of Psychology* 53, 1–25.

Turner, W. 1972. Stanford vetoes Shockley course. *New York Times*, 9.

VanOefflen, M., and P. Vos. 1984. The young child's processing of dot patterns. *International Journal of Behavioral Development* 7: 53–66.

Vygotsky, L. S. 1930. *Mind in society: The development of higher mental process*, edited by M. Cole. Reprint, Cambridge, Mass.: Harvard University Press, 1978.

————. 1934. *Thought and language*, edited and translated by E. Hanfmann and G. Vakar. Reprint, Cambridge, Mass.: MIT Press, 1962.

Watson, J. B. 1930. *Behaviorism*. Chicago, Ill.: University of Chicago Press.

Wechsler, D. 1989. *Manual for the Wechsler preschool and primary scale of intelligence-Revised* (WPPSI-R). San Antonio, Tex.: Psychological Corporation.

Weissberg, R., H. A. Ruff, and K. R. Lawson. 1990. The usefulness of reaction time tasks in studying attention and organization of behavior in young children. *Journal of Developmental and Behavioral Pediatrics* 11: 59–64.

Wellman, H. M. 1977, March. Tip of the tongue and feeling of knowing experiences: A developmental study of memory monitoring. *Child Development*, 48, 1, 13–21.

Werker, J., and P. J. McLeod. 1989. Infant preference for both male and female infant-directed talk: A developmental study of attentional and affective responsiveness. *Canadian Journal of Psychology* 43: 230–46.

White, A. R. 1964. *Attention*. Oxford: Blackwell.

Widner, R. L. 1996. The effects of demand characteristics on the reporting of tip-of-the-tongue and feeling-of-knowing states. *The American Journal of Psychology* 109, no. 4: 525–39.

Wiggins, G. 1998. *Educative assessment: Designing assessment to inform and improve student performance*. San Francisco: Jossey-Bass.

Williams, J. 2001. The effectiveness of spontaneous attention to form. *System* 29, no. 3: 325–40.

Wolberg, L. R. 1967. *Short-term psychotherapy*. New York: Grune and Stratton.

Wolf, T. H. 1973. *Alfred Binet*. Chicago, Ill.: University of Chicago Press.

Wolfram, W., and E. R. Thomas. 2002. *The development of African American English*. Oxford, England: Blackwell Publishers.

Wright, J. W. 1995. *The universal almanac*. Kansas City, Mo.: Andrews and McMeel.

Yates, B. T., and W. Mischel. 1979. Young children's preferred attention strategies for delaying gratification. *Journal of Personality and Social Psychology* 37: 286–300.

Yondo, R., and J. Kogan. 1968. *The effects of task complexity on reflection–impulsivity*. York: Macmillan.

Zaner, R., and D. Ihde. 1973. *Phenomenology and existentialism*. New York: Putnam.

About the Author

Harry Morgan received a bachelor's degree from New York University in education, a master's degree in social work from the University of Wisconsin, Madison, and a doctorate in early childhood education from the University of Massachusetts, Amherst.

Professor Morgan has taught at Bank Street College, the University of New Hampshire, Ohio University, Syracuse University, and is currently a professor of curriculum and instruction at the University of West Georgia.

His books include *The Learning Community* (1973), *Historical Perspectives on the Education of Black Children* (1995), *Cognitive Styles and Classroom Learning* (1997), and *The Imagination of Early Childhood Education* (1999), and his work was included in the Carl Rogers's editions of *Studies of the Person*.

Professor Morgan's research has appeared in *Social Policy* (1980), *The Roeper Review* (1996), *The Journal of Educational Research* (1995), *Research in Middle Level Education* (2000), and *The Negro Educational Review* (2002).

Currently, Dr. Morgan teaches and supervises graduate studies in child development, learning theory, critical race theory, language acquisition, curriculum development, and educational research.